26.$\underline{95}$

Lay-out:
Michael Prasuhn, BDG, 4800 Bielefeld 1
Drawings:
Evelyn Prasuhn, 4800 Bielefeld 11
Translation:
Albert J. Thiel, Norwalk/USA
Printing:
Werbedruck Zünkler, 4800 Bielefeld 11
1st Edition 1986

AD aquadocumenta Verlag

Albert J. Thiel, 1943, born in Antwerp, Belgium, mastered
in Economics and Finance from St. Ignatius University.
Aquarist since childhood, he has after many years of fresh
water tropical fish keeping, devoted uncountable
hours to water chemistry and the marine aquarium. His
views and present beliefs were originally formatted by the
extensive research done by Stephen Spotte, Vice President
Sea Research Foundation Inc., and Director Mystic
Marinelife Aquarium, Mystic, Connecticut, whom he
wishes to acknowledge.
Presently Albert Thiel is involved in research on marine
Macro-Algae and the feasibility of growing them in Sea
water home Aquariums, as well as their influence on water
chemistry, and the reciprocal effect such algae have on
marine fish and invertebrae life.
Albert Thiel wishes to thank his wife Sarah for her
understanding and patience. Without her help this task
would not have been achieved in the time frame required.
He also wants to thank Karen Loazia for having participated
in translation.

Kaspar Horst / Horst E. Kipper

The Optimum Aquarium

The sure way to success.

Guide for the installation and care of the
Fresh Water Aquarium

About this Book

This book is the result of a long and close cooperation between Kaspar Horst and Horst Kipper, and already has quite a history. The ideas behind its development and content were laid down by Kaspar Horst and Horst Kipper in the 1960's.

The techniques used to keep tropical fish and plants in aquariums, have gone through enormous changes after the Second World War. Correct lighting, adequate water movement, the availability of plants and fertilizer were now within everyone's easy reach, and technically possible. The Aquarist is now able to keep and maintain a nice looking aquarium. He did however also often experience the contrary. By not paying attention to nature's laws and water quality requirements, even modern techniques can result in more harm than good.

Many Aquarists failed to understand the connection between light (energy) and nutrients added to the water. Several rather complicated chemical processes, as for instance changes in the pH of the water, changes in the nitrogen cycle course, can have very dire consequences if not properly controlled. Problems with algae, plants that are not growing although fertilizer is administered dying and diseased fish, have in many cases been the experience of a good number of Aquarists.

As a result of this inability to maintain the proper quality of life for fish and plants, many Aquarists emptied their aquariums, stored them somewhere in their garage or basements, or they ended up with and amongst all the other junk stored somewhere in the house or apartment.

Obviously, information on how to

use modern techniques to keep an aquarium with plants and fish, were not as readily available to the aquarists, as one would have hoped.

Kaspar Horst and Horst Kipper detected that there was a mission for them to fulfill in this area. They decided to analyze the connections between water quality at the sites where the fish were actually being caught, and where the plants were growing, return with multiple samples of the water and of the substrate of the rivers and lakes, and in general of the various fish and plant biotopes. These samples were then analyzed in the laboratory, numerous notes were taken and an enormous amount of data collected in this fashion. This data was then later used when trying to raise and grow numerous types of aquarium plants.

After many attempts and numerous experiments, they developed a very comprehensive and hobbyist-orientated set of rules for the keeping of tropical fish and plants.

In 1977 they decided to write the fruit of their work down, and publish it in the form of a book, »The Perfect Aquarium« which was published by »Tetra«. The way this book was received was just astonishing. Professional publishers and authors alike were amazed. A first edition of 20 000 copies, large for the aquarium field, sold out in just a few months. A second edition followed soon thereafter, and within two years the third edition appeared on the market. This book was an Aquaristic bestseller right from its publication!

This was proof that Horst Kipper and Kaspar Horst had laid their finger on something which was really missing in the available literature, and a book for which all Aquarists had been waiting. The name »Perfect Aquarium« also became synonymous with a nice looking and efficiently run aquarium.

Time however goes on. The Tropical Fish Keeping described in the first two editions was developed using the products and technique available at that time. The authors however continued to work, and perfected many of the available techniques and measuring devices.

Today approximately 8 years after the publication of the first edition, the authors present a completely revised edition of the book, with the addition of numerous new chapters, describing in detail the latest techniques available in Tropical Fish Keeping. This time however the book is being published by Aquadocumenta Verlag.

The authors are thankful to Tetra that, freed of their obligation to them, they were able to adapt the book change what needed to be changed, add what seemed necessary at this particular junction in the hobby, and delete techniques and recommendations which in light of recent developments did not seem adequate anymore.

The new title selected »The Optimum Aquarium«, is to be seen as an enhancement made possible due to these developments, a natural progression in the techniques described in the »Perfect Aquarium«.

aquadocumenta Verlag
Bielefeld, October 1985

Content

Content

Content

Introduction

Without fear of exageration one can say that in the last ten years the keeping of tropical and ornamental fish in aquariums and ponds, has grown considerably, and all over the world. Not only in Germany, where according to recent statistics 1 25 million households are keeping aquariums, but also in other European countries, in the U.S.A., in Japan, in Australia and in many Asian countries, has the keeping of tropical fish become more than just a hobby. Fifteen years ago it is estimated that there were approximately 700 000 Aquarists in Germany. Today, if we include those who keep gold fish and a number of home fish and carp koi, the number is in excess of 1.6 million.

Comparative figures for other countries are unfortunately not available. In Thailand however we know that there are over 100 000 Hobbyists, and that in Bangkok alone, every week, 150 000 tropical fish are being sold. Of the 300 pet-shops in Thailand more than a 150 are in Bangkok. These are really amazing numbers even if the keeping of ornamental fish is a tradition in Thailand.

The substantial number of Hobbyist's magazines in the U.S.A., Japan and the U.K. are proof that the interest in tropical fish keeping has really grown considerably. This also allows us to deny the rumor that circulates from time to time that the keeping of tropical fish is not much more than a fad.

Of course, the way in which the hobby is being practiced differs in each individual country. Proof of that is the fact that plastic plants and many little decorative divers skulls etc. are still being used in certain countries. Perhaps the reason for these differences has to do on one hand with the lack of available literature and guidelines, and the lack of adequate products on the other, especially in the United States. One of the attempts made by this book is to change this situation, since the book not only will be published in German but also in English.

Notwithstanding the differences, it is clear to us that the serious hobbyists make up the greater majority, and that the interest in keeping tropical fish and plants in a professional manner is much stronger than it appears on the surface. The authors of this book are attempting by its publication in other languages, to contribute in their own way to the dissemination of information that up to now has only been available in German. At the same time the authors know that in doing so they will give the keeping of tropical fish the necessary impulse to take a more professional direction. We can however not lose sight of the fact that this growing interest in the keeping of tropical fish, only represents a portion of the total art of keeping domestic animals. It does require however a much more intensive analyses and a much greater amount of care than is the case for those keeping other domestic animals.

We do not wish to let this statement stand without proof and risk the strong reaction of those keeping birds, dogs, cats and other animals. Unlike for instance dogs, which live in immediate contact with their masters, fish have to exist in water. Water in this respect is still a much foreign element. Over the aeons the human race has slowly but surely evolved in such a way that it has been removed further and further from the natural element that water is. We could of course not exist without the presence and a certain degree of closeness to water, however water is not part of the primary habitat, as is the case for tropical and ornamental fish. As a result the Aquarist has to engage himself in a much more intensive way in trying to duplicate the habitat of his fish. This requires a greater dedication to the hobby, as would be the case with Hobbyists keeping dogs, birds, cats and other animals, especially since the habitat in which the fish live is so different from what the Hobbyists is used to, and so much more complicated to maintain at the required levels of quality.

1.1.

The Optimum Aquarium: Claim and Objectives

No doubt many will find it daring to call a book »The Optimum Aquarium«, indeed what in our world is optimal, what is perfect? Oscar Wild's aphorism: »Perfect is only that what can be achieved without effort,« seems to exclude an Optimum Aquarium.

Every Hobbyist knows how much time, effort and care he has to devote to his aquarium.

Even those who do not have an aquarium understand that water does not remain pure without care, fish don't stay alive without the addition of well balanced food and nourishment, and plants do not thrive in the absence of fertilizer. And so on. Something needs to be done for or to an aquarium all the time.

From this it would appear that tropical fish keeping is the most labor intensive hobby around.

That it is however not the case. On the other hand, and it should be said, it is not a hobby that can be practiced successfully without any effort. It is, as we already said, a hobby where: attention to creating nature-like conditions, willingness to learn, care and attention, a certain amount of practice and experience obtained over time, are necessary if one wishes their tank not just to be a splashing pool but a nature-like biotope for tropical freshwater fish and plants.

This claim becomes more meaningful with the degree of influence the keeper wishes to imprint on the changes that take place in this habitat. And a stronger influence than the transport of fish and plants, halfway around the world as in e.g. from the Amazones, or Thailand or Malaysia to Europe, is hard to imagine.

When one agrees with this way of thinking, then the interest in keeping tropical fish goes hand in hand with the duty to provide the fish and plants, arbitrarily removed from their living areas, with a biotope that is not just an acceptable approximation, but rather with a close replica of the natural habitat that those fish and plants originally came from. The closer this habitat simulates the natural one, the better the Hobbyist has lived up to the mission he has taken upon himself when entering the hobby.

We the authors, Kaspar Horst and Horst Kipper (who have been involved for over 30 years with the practical keeping of aquariums, have researched on natural habitats, investigated the requirements of fish and plant life, looking at questions dealing with water chemistry problems involved in reproducing natural biotopes) are of the opinion that the only way for a hobbyist to increase his professionalism over his hobby, is through continuously striving for Optimum Conditions.

To be a true Aquarist represents, in our opinion, more than just knowing the conditions fish and plants require to survive, but rather to acknowledge them, and to do all that is possible to duplicate them. Every Hobbyist, should therefore see it as his mission and duty to create optimum aquarium conditions, to live up to the task that he has taken upon himself.

1.2.
The Optimum Aquarium: Wishful Thinking or Fact?

Having set forth our views, and a model outlining the basic laws governing the keeping of tropical fish and plants, it should not come as a surprise that a number of people will reject these views outright, or label it as wishful thinking.

It is likely that many Aquarists reading these lines, although they have been trying to maintain a successful aquarium, have regularly encountered disappointments. And their skepticism about our suggestions is therefore understandable. Indeed their reaction might be to think that »here are another two experts arriving on the scene, claiming to have finally discovered the formula for the optimum aquarium.«

From the many conversations with Hobbyists we have had, we know that the desire to own a well running aquarium is very often laced with failures, and not infrequently accompanied by resignation at the many problems which often seem insurmountable. This is hardly surprising for there have been, and still are, often contradictory suggestions made in the literature that is generally available. To be successful in light of the many discrepancies that one can find, and the contradictory suggestions on how to maintain an aquarium, often requires a good deal of luck at the same time.

As nice as luck is, it is also rare. Unfortunately, luck has the disadvantage that it cannot be repeated at will. We, the authors of this book, would like to make it possible for Aquarists, not to have to depend on their luck, but instead be able to refer to and build on knowledge that is available to them, knowledge that has been tested in thousands of experiments. For only then can good results be obtained. The question whether the Optimum Aquarium is wishful thinking or fact, can be most simply answered by using the suggestions made in this book and daring to set up a new aquarium, or modify the present one and deciding on the answer to the question by judging the results obtained. In doing so, even the most skeptical aquarium owner will be convinced that the establishment, and maintainence of such a habitat is not wishful thinking but indeed fact.

1 Bad example: Unattractive aquarium, with airstone, few plants and hazy water.
2 Good example: Densely planted and well appointed aquarium. Fast growing plants ensure the supply of oxygen, no airstone, clear water.

1

2

1.3.

A Habitat with its own Laws: The Aquarium

In our work over the years, we have clearly established that, contrary to earlier notions and beliefs, water plants are not just decoration or border markings, or frames through which to view the fish. Healthy and thriving plants are the elementary biological requirement for an optimum fresh water aquarium. To us, the »recognition« of the significance of water plants, is the »missing link« in aquarium maintainance to date. Our strong belief in this statement is the result of years of scientific research. The experiments were conducted in our laboratories as a permanent series of tests and experiments with the latest chemical and physical arrangements possible, with results from countless expeditions to examine and analyze natural habitats. Last but not least it is also the result of the support of major chemical laboratories (Asta-Werke AG, Degussa, Dupla, Tetra-Werke) and many scientists with whom we have become friendly over the years, amongst others Professor Dr. Rolf Geisler, and Dr. Eberhard Stengel, who have encouraged and assisted us, time and time again, and with advice have motivated us in pursuing this laboring intensive effort.

That is the way through which it was possible for us, to arrive at knowledge that could be directly, or some even indirectly, transferred to the artificial habitat that an aquarium is.

As important as the research done in the Tropics is, it is only through the scientific analyses conducted in our laboratories that we were able to arrive at demonstrating their general relevance to the keeping of tropical fish and plants. Through the studies done in our labs, and put forth in this book, we are able to say that they are valid for all fresh water aquariums. By offering guidelines that are generally applicable, and readily reproduceable, we are able to claim unequivocally that it is possible to create an »Optimum Aquarium«. For example, it would be wrong to transfer analyses obtained from nature directly to the aquarium. Rather, one must first translate these data and results in a set of guidelines and rules, that are practical and usable by the Aquarist, in everyday care.

This can easily be demonstrated by the following example: many tropical waters are particularly soft and low in dissolved salts. A total hardness of less than 1° dH (1 degree German hardness) = 17 ppm CaO of hardness and a conductivity of between 20 and 30 μS are not uncommon. One could not keep an aquarium with these conditions for very long, as it would be too unstable. In this respect the major difference between natural and artifical habitats becomes noticeable. Even though the level of dissolved oxygen in natural waters is low, (for example between 2 and 5 ml/l) this cannot lead us to the conclusion that this would be an acceptable value for an aquarium. To the contrary such a low level of dissolved oxygen would very quickly kill off a substantial number of fish. Not only fish, but the aquarium and its contents itself need much higher amounts of oxygen. That level is usually situated close to the saturation point of dissolved oxygen in water. Besides fish, bacteria above all, require oxygen in order to metabolize and process the waste which accumulates in the aquarium during the day (from feeding, plants, and fish waste). From these examples we can see that it is not enough to just imitate or duplicate natural water, instead one must acquire the knowledge on how to create an artificial aquarium habitat, using what we find in nature as a basis.

Since the first edition of this book, more than 7 years ago, we have been able to observe a definite sophistication in the keeping of tropical fish, frequently accompanied by success. Through the concepts advocated in our first book, plants and fish can now be kept much more successfully. The market for an ideal aquarium has now become so large, that the industry can afford to develop large fish and plant production sites. This enables aquarium fanciers to obtain a larger number, and a wider variety of plants from specialty pet stores. This trend is further supported by the ever improving synthetic foods of all forms.

As a result of these developments, a practical environmental protection plan came about, which will have far reaching consequences. Through the creation of the Optimum Aquarium we will succeed in living up to those standards.

Bielefeld, January 1986.

Kaspar Horst   Horst E. Kipper

2.
Stock Taking

A book dealing with the latest techniques and findings in Tropical Fish Keeping could not be complete, if it did not deal with at least a short retrospective of our wonderful hobby. In this way one can explain and understand the developments and the unfolding of new techniques by comparing the past, the present and the future.

2.1.
Historical Retrospective

The gold fish bowl was introduced to Europe from China as early as the 17th century. It was not until the 19th century however, approximately in the year 1850, that the aquarium – originating in England – became a popular room decoration on the Continent. Around that time under the influence of the German teacher Rossmaessler, the keeping of tropical fish, although it was not referred to with that name at that time, began to adopt the rectangular shaped containers, which we today know. Until that time it had been customary to keep fish in round or spherical containers.

Keeping tropical or ornamental fish, which even today is not without its problems, as we all know, must have been quite imperfect in those days, especially in view of the nonexistant technical advice, literature and other sources of information that we can now rely on. Back then one could be happy if, as a nature

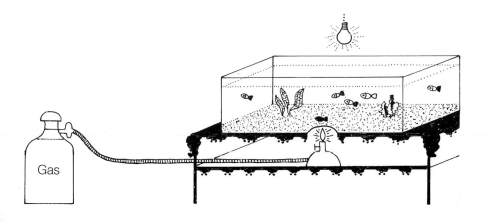

1 Salon aquarium from the early times of the hobby. Aquaristics started with the »open« aquarium about 100 years ago. Light hoods then closed the top of the aquarium for several decades. Nowadays, modern aquaristic again allows easy access from the top.
2 A 95 year old aquarium in the »Das Alte Aquarium«-Museum.

lover or a lover of plants and fish, one was able to obtain just a few specimens from the tropics.

One must also bear in mind that fish and plants had to come from great distances across entire continents and endure month long sea voyages. In that way, of course, a natural selection already took place, which permitted only the hardiest specimens to arrive more or less well preserved in London, Bremen or Hamburg. Whatever was still alive when getting to its final destination really only needed to be adapted to the changed living conditions in Europe. That is of course easy to say but let us take a closer look at what these conditions in fact were.

Systematic research did not exist. One could only observe what was happening in nature and try to replicate it as close as possible in the aquarium. Just one example: compost and sand were mixed and used as substrate, because one wanted to provide enough nourishment for the plants, as in nature. Insufficient heaters were installed under the aquarium in order to produce warm tropical water temperature. Filter and filtration techniques were totally nonexistant, and as the water became turbid it had to be changed very frequently, in many cases every couple of days. Lighting consisted of simple light bulbs, which could only provide the plants with a minimal, too low, amount of light. Surprisingly, these totally inadequate living conditions were not as catastrophic for the aquarium of the time as one might believe. Thus for example, the rich ground that was used provided a good amount of fertilizer including carbonic acid, that the aquatic plants could assimilate and metabolize. Water circulation, through the substrate, was aided by heat through the bottom, while the weak light prevented the plants from overmetabolizing. As a reasult, the carbon dioxide (CO_2) consumption in these aquariums was not particularly high.

Through the necessary and frequent changes of water, new nutrients were constantly being supplied to the aquarium, while on the other hand toxic or hazardous substances, which might have developed in the aquarium, were being removed. Besides, the tap water back then was considerably better than it is today. Due to the absence of environmental pollution, the amounts of nitrogen compounds and nitrates being added to the water were minimal.

It was thus possible at the end of the 19th century and beginning of the 20th, for the keeping of tropical fish to develop, and while we might no longer consider it as such, contribute a great deal to the knowledge that we have at the present day, even though the techniques used then are no longer being practiced. They were the stepping stones, so to speak, that lead to the modern way of tropical fish and plant keeping, as it is being practiced in the 1980's.

2.2.
Aquariums Today
2.2.1.
Tank Dimensions

We all know that in the field of Tropical Fish Keeping many things have changed over the years, and this is especially so with regard to tank dimensions. Size, color and type of wood – if any – used, are selected to match the furnishings of the rooms in which these aquariums will be placed. There is of course nothing wrong with that, except that we determined that the »short side« dimensions of aquariums are usually too small. The reason for this is on one hand the normalisation of furniture measurements, and on the other that are attempts with a small investment to obtain as large as possible an aquarium front view impact. This then translates into possibly high and narrow aquariums.

Many architects are proud to present their clients with aquariums that look nice but frequently are much too high. The realization of these mistakes unfortunately come only once the aquarium has been attached to a wall as a permanent fixture, has been started up, filled with water, and has now become an item that can no longer be moved. Nobody seems to have thought about the fact that such an aquarium can never be properly lit and also that it is very hard to tend to, because of its depth.

This is also resulted in tanks that no longer conform to standard lengths of fluorescent tubes (see chapters 3.2 and 3.9). It should be pointed out in this respect that this is much more so in Europe than it is in the United States, where although the problem still exists, standardization is much greater than overseas.

2.2.2.
Substrate

In setting up an aquarium there are still many techniques used today, which for reasons not clearly understood, make the mistake of trying to save on depth or thickness of the substrate. The fact that aquatic plants have to spread their roots is often not taken into consideration. Furthermore different types of fertilizers e.g. potting soil with imaginary additives is used, resulting in a substrate that is so compacted that oxygen depletion quickly occurs, with the resulting blackening of the substrate, and anaerobic bacteria activity. Even today one can buy additives claiming many many years of success, all promising lush plant growth without much effort. In fact, these soil mixtures frequently consists of, for example, a large part of compost and clay and other such fertilizing agents not suited for the aquarium. Other fertilizers which are regularly used in agriculture are added. The result is indeed an exuberant lush growth of plants, but also an immediate plague of algae, right from the early days on. Such substrates cannot be used in aquariums. (In this connection please refer to Chapter 3.4 in which this subject is discussed more in detail.)

2.2.3.
The Water

Aqua is the latin name for water, and aquarium, also derived from latin, stands for water container. Water is also the habitat in which the fish and plants must live.

If the reader questions the fact that we are only addressing the subject matter of water at this particular time, it does not mean that we do not consider water less important than the other subjects touched upon, however we wish to address the various matters to be covered in a systematic way. When one sets up an aquarium, the substrate is obviously added to the aquarium before the water. For that reason we are only ad-

1 Through many sprayers the CO_2 is removed from the water. View of a modern spraying chamber of a Water Works operation.

1

dressing it at this stage. Water is a subject that we will be discussing at great length. We are only touching the surface right now.

Anyone who has set up an aquarium will quickly realize that water is not just water and that all waters are not the same. Water is characterized by the dissolved components that it contains. These can be gasses, salts, minerals and trace elements. The way these interact and the quantities it contains also determine the way in which the plants and fish will fare in that water.

It is the practice nowadays to fill aquariums with mains water. This is the first problem that we need to address. Most likely your Water Authority certifies that the water your are using is bacteria free and drinkable, this does however not mean that this water is suited for aquarium use. To the contrary.

Laws governing the quality of water that is delivered vary greatly. In order to deliver water that conforms to the various laws in effect, water treatment plants have to purify this water to such an extent that because of all the processes used, the water is so sterile that no plants can be grown in it, mainly because all fertilizing agents have been removed.

It is also the concern of many Water Works that the water they deliver might damage the pipes and other conduits through which it flows if the water is too aggressive. To remedy this water works treat your water in

	Spring Water	Mains water in the same local
pH	7.2	7.4
Evaporation residue	710 mg/l	680 mg/l
Total alkalinity (ccm 1/10 n Acid/100 ccm)	6.6 mg/l	
Carbonate hardness (Acid binding Capacity)	18.5°dH	16.8°dH
Total hardness	14.0°dH	14.0°dH
Bound CO_2	145 mg/l	132 mg/l
Free CO_2	59.4 mg/l	35.2 mg/l
Aggressive Carbonic Acid	0 mg/l	0 mg/l
Chlorides	71 mg/l	52 mg/l
Sulfates	140 mg/l	188 mg/l
Ammonia	0.1 mg/l	0 mg/l
Nitrite	0 mg/l	0 mg/l
Nitrate	22 mg/l	24 mg/l
Iron	1.7 mg/l	0 mg/l
Manganese	0.2 mg/l	0 mg/l
Phosphate	0.1 mg/l (less)	0 mg/l
Potassium permanganate consumption	12 mg/l	4 mg/l

various ways which unfortunately all negatively influence its quality, and reduce its usefullness for the aquarium. For instance, most of the dissolved compounds which frequently are removed are exactly those which are beneficial to plants e.g. phosphates, iron, manganese, aluminium are all removed before the water is delivered to your house or apartment. When reducing the aggressiveness of the water, because for instance it contains too much free CO_2, the latter is partly or completely removed, depending on the level of carbonate hardness.

Carbon dioxide however is the most important nutrient the plants require. This is not all yet: through floculation important organics, present either in solution or as free floating particles, are precipitated and removed.

The increased use of well water and the pollution of open waters contribute to the fact that the water we now use contains other elements undesirable. This results, in the aquarium, in over-fertilization through excess nitrates (nitrogen over-fertilization) and excess phosphates.

Lastly the chemical composition of the water, differing geologically (e.g. hardness) also has to be taken into consideration.

The chemical composition of the water you are getting will always be different from the chemical composition of the water in which the plants grow. When we take this into consideration, bad plant growth and disease are the most common result. How much public water authorities change our water can be seen on page 22, in a comparison used here as an example only.

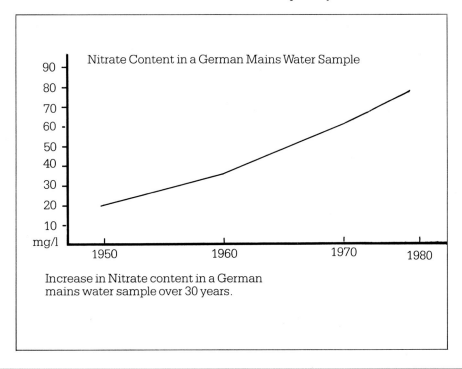

Increase in Nitrate content in a German mains water sample over 30 years.

We have also discovered during our research that the real problems only begin once the water analyses has been completed, as it is our experience that many Aquarists really do not know what to do with the figures they obtain. Literature is of not much help in this respect as we find that it contains many inaccuracies. For instance many texts one can find and refer to, still explain total hardness as the sum of the sulfate and carbonate hardnesses. Aquarists are not aware of the fact that carbonate hardness is directly related to the pH of the water that is being analyzed. Aquarists are also not aware of the fact that carbon is a very important fertilizer needed by all plants. The only thing the aquarist seems to know is that overdosage of carbon dioxide can poison the fish.

Water quality also suffers from the fact that the aquarist believe that old, or aged water, possesses superior qualities, and that Aquarists seem to think that the older the water, the better it is. Another mistake frequently made is that the biological filters that are advocated on the market are in most cases much too small, and that when one reads the advertisements for certain of these products, some even claim to eliminate water changes completely, or just about completely.

What we do know however is that most fish, and practically all plants, come from areas where the water quality is far superior to anything that can be found in an aquarium. It is for instance a fact that in the tropical regions, where fish and plants come from, the water in which the fish swim and the plants grow is replaced approximately 100 times per hour.

Just a last word about aged water. Aged water is really only of benefit in as much as we can at least be sure that here all the chlorine and chloramine has been removed. It is also not the kind of water that we desire to use from a pH standpoint. We also know nowadays that yellow and brownish coloration that such water has, comes from the leaching into the water of various substances that, supposedly inert materials in the tank, release. Such substances are nepharious for both fish and plants.

It is better to forget everything we have heard about aged water and start anew. Please be reminded of this section next time you do a water change. Later in this book (chapter 3.5) we will go more into detail about water quality.

2.2.4.
Filtration, Aeration, Water Movement

Since we have now filled our aquarium with water every aquarist will ask himself what to do next about filtration, aeration and water movement, and whether they are necessary. First of all let us answer this with an unqualified »yes«. This is also the present opinion of the all Hobbyists. Is this way of thinking also the right one? We shall see. Let us begin with the airstones which can be found in 95 % of all present day freshwater aquariums. Whether you believe it or not, such airstones shatter every attempt to keep an optimum aquarium.

Aeration of aquariums does add oxygen to the water, no doubt about it. On the other hand, at the same time, it removes most of the carbon dioxide that is dissolved in the water, with the resulting damage to the plants who need it. As a result of removing the carbon dioxide the pH of the water will rise, and Aquarists will try to take measures to reduce it to acceptable levels. As a result of the lack of carbon dioxide, plants cannot perform the metabolic processes that they are supposed to in a proper manner. This results in stunted plant growth, and reduces the plants ability to provide or to release oxygen in the water, for the benefit of the fish.

The addition of mineral, or seltzer water, only brings temporary help as in a very short period of time the aeration also removes the dissolved carbon dioxide in such mineral waters, while at the same time increasing the

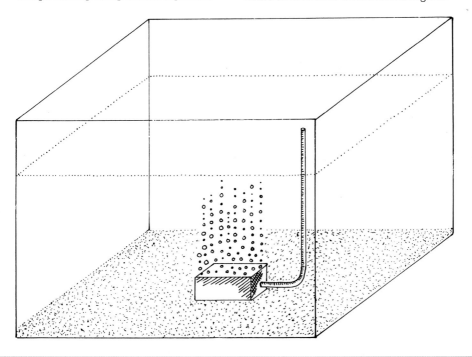

amount of dissolved minerals to too high a level, increasing the »salts« content beyond acceptable limits. Aquarists are confused by methods that are neither serious nor proven, as for instance reducing the flow of water in the through substrate. Special lamps are being offered which supposedly allow the surface water to circulate, through special condiuts through the substrate. Seeing is believing is what one thing required in this case.

Filtration of the water is obviously meaningful, but doing so through the use of filters that are air driven has a number of drawbacks. Air bubbles in the aquarium are not desirable if they are removing, as a side effect, the dissolved carbon dioxide which is necessary for the plants. Most of the air driven filters available on the market unfortunately operate in this fashion,

and we do not advocate the use of such filters to those who wish to maintain plants in their aquarium.

Undergravel filters are nowadays still popular. They are used especially in fish-only aquariums, e. g. in commercial set-ups. We know however today, that water does not pass through these filters uniformally (color test is convincing enough). As a result zones of different oxygen concentration occur in the substrate, which are in both cases unfavorable for plant growth.

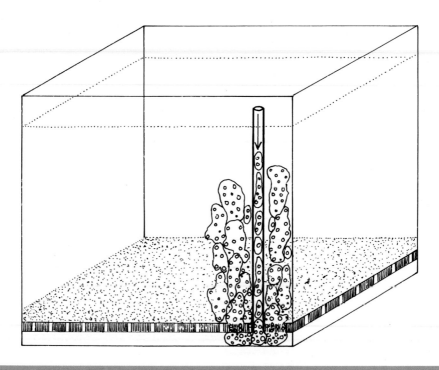

Even the undergravel filters which are so frequently advocated, do not have a place in the Optimum Aquarium. Indeed, on one hand we can never be sure exactly where the water passes through the gravel (water always finds the way of least resistance and a color test will demonstrate this quite easily), and on the other hand water flowing through the area where the plants root certainly does not promote growth, as indeed a constant flow of water over the root system increases the amount of oxygen in the substrate to a degree which is undesirable.

Along the same lines it is no longer necessary in every case to use all the additives that are being placed in box or cannister filters, indeed certain filter media will darken the water, ion exchangers create an uncontrollable process in the water, and this has a negative impact on the sensitive system that an aquarium is. Coral sand and other calcium-rich stone used, increases the total and carbonate hardness of the water beyond the point that we may require it.

Here again we refer you to a later chapter, where we deal much more in detail with this matter. (Chapter 3.5.)

2.2.5.
Plants Fertilization and Care

We have now progressed to the point in the set up of our aquarium that we can deal with the subject of plants. It has already been pointed out, in the section dealing with substrates used in aquarium, that many Aquarists have attempted to set up so called »Dutch« aquarium. Unfortunately these Aquarists are the exception rather than the rule.

It has been our observation that in most case Aquarists have a tendency not to put enough plants in their aquariums.

A few plants in the corners and perhaps a few plants in the back seem to be the rule. Right in the middle of the aquarium, as if it were the attention getter, the most expensive plant will be found. This is without regard for the fact whether these plant grows tall or bushy, or require a lot or little light. It seems as if the status symbol needs to be in plain view, and that the Aquarist finds the middle of the aquarium seems to be the most adequate place to achieve this. Plants are selected arbitrarily. It is also not uncommon to find plants in aquariums which are not aquatic plants, and which will unfortunately not survive for very long if submersed. Such plants also do not participate in the chemical and organic compound exchanges taking place in the water, and as such do not contribute to its quality. Once these plants die off, they are one more reason for disappointment. Another factor to which we wish to draw attention, is the weekly or bi-weekly addition of fertilizer, without changing a portion of the water, or without regard for the acutal fertilization requirements of the plants. Such practices are, in view of today's knowledge, no longer acceptable, as they do not take the requirements of the plants into account, and also not the peaks and valleys in fertilization concentrations.

The addition of tablets that release carbon dioxide (CO_2) in the water are also part of what we would like ro refer to as antiquated Tropical Fish Keeping, and continuing this practise set back the quality of standards used by the Aquarists, to the Stone Age.

Lighting provided for the plants, and its effects on growth, are too often reglected, partly through a lack of knowledge and a combination of lack of knowledge and time. Such maintainence techniques can certainly not be part of what we advocate is necessary to maintain an optimum aquarium. We will deal with this subject much more in detail in Chapter 3.6.

It is still not being recognised nowadays, that the best water quality is obtained in an aquarium that is densely planted. Often too much importance is given to the decorative impact of single plants. Even the plants suffer, as it is a fact that they grow better in groups.

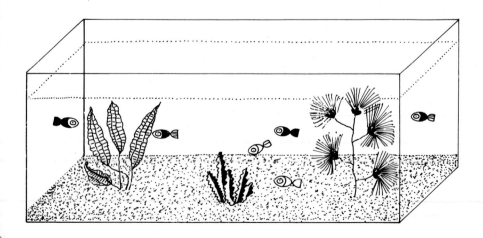

2.2.6.
Fish and Plants

The fish found in aquariums as they are kept today, are in the true sense of the word a chapter unto themselves.

In most cases too many fish are placed in an aquarium, so many that we could in fact nearly dispense with the heater as the fish can keep each other warm. Often also, fish that are not compatible are being mixed in one and the same aquarium. Aquarists who wish to keep plants include in their selection fish that disturb the substrate, and which are obviously not the right selection if one wishes to maintain a nice and healthy growth of aquatic plants.

Some people even select fish for purely aesthetical reasons, for instance 2 blue, 3 black, 4 green, 5 red, etc. This is done without any concern for the requirements of the fish, or which fish can be mixed together in a community aquarium.

In this context, one has to take notice of something that is of basic importance when dealing with Fish and Plants, especially because it enters into the picture when taking stock of TODAY'S AQUARIUM. Although both come from places far away, most fish and plants can now be in Europe and the U.S.A. within a maximum of 20 hours. In the past fish were being caught in their natural biotope and flown to these areas' distributors. With the increased interest in both fish and plants it has become economically feasible to open plant farms in various countries, and to get involved in the commercial raising of many types of tropical fish. Based on our research, it appears that the majority of the fish that are being offered for sale today in our pet-shop are now raised in captivity. European breeders send an average of 3 million fish per year to German, American, African and even to Saudi Arabian wholesalers for resale to local Hobbyists. Of course there is a very positive aspect to the artificial breeding of fish, as it has stopped or greatly reduced the depletion of the natural wild stock. Nature is no longer a self service for the Hobbyist, and we certainly are in favour of this trend. The natural biotopes however are still being threatened by industrialization, the building of new roads and deforestation.

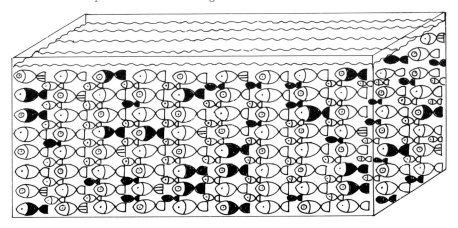

On the other hand, fish which are bred in captivity, e.g. angel fish from South America, are flown to Asia where they are bred in captivity, then flown back to South America and later sold as wild caught fish. This is how we find wild caught, bred in Hong-Kong, South American fish

Fish and how they get here		
	Living area	Catching station, 2–3 days
	Holding Station	3–4 weeks
	Exporter	14 days and 20 hours flight
	Breeder	6 month flight 20 hours
	Importer	Breeding, 1–2 weeks
	Whole-saler	1–2 weeks
	Pet-Shop	1–3 weeks
	Hobbyist	1–30 days

1 Fish counting for export.
2 Large fish export installation of a decorative fish breeder in Thailand.

which we then appear for sale in Europe, and Hobbyists believe that they are paying for a wild-caught fish. The same seems to apply to plants,

1

2

which grown in Singapore, Bangkok or Indonesia need to be artificially over-fertilized, as the growers wish to speed up their readiness for resale in

our countries, as quickly as possible. Such plants are unfortunately not of the type of quality that we would like to see, and cannot sustain and adapt themselves to our water. In addition they often arrive with spores attached to them, which under good fertilization conditions in our aquariums, bloom and infest the tank with undesirable algae plagues. It is also the cause for the introduction of snails from the wild (especially from Singapore and Sri Lanka).

Today we know that aquatic plants from Sri Lanka and for instance Borneo, require different survival and growth factors. Because the water from our mains is closer in composition to that from Ceylon, the chances of keeping such plants heal-thy are much greater. Unfortunately, as a result of this, many Cryptocoryne areas in Sri Lanka have been depleted of plants. This has resulted in strong efforts to prohibit future exports of wild plants from Sri Lanka. As a result of such actions, but also for economic reasons large plant farms have sprung up in Singapore, Thailand. Such farms are being planned even in Australia.

Also in Europe one can find large plant farms, as for instance in Denmark. One of the largest can be found near Aarhus on Jutland. Despite higher energy and personnel costs they are competitive with the Asian operations. Since these plants are cultivated from stock originating in Europe they are very well suited for our aquariums.

Today there are already many ornamental fish establishments and import stations which have taken it upon themselves to eliminate the instability and susceptibility to illness of imported fish. This involves chang-

1 One of the largest plant farms in Europe. Many aquarium plants, here Anubias, are precultivated »emers«. The transition to aquarium plant is easier as a result.

1

ing the diets and lengthy quarantine periods. Similarly the breeding of ornamental or tropical fish is nowadays praticed according to the latest available techniques.

In the meantime there is a worldwide coalition of international exporters and ornamental/tropical fish breeders for whom it is principle to halt the depletion of nature and natural habitats, and promote planned cultivation of fish and plants. Naturally, operations both at home and abroad are not always 100 % successful.

Why, should we ask ourselves, are imported fish from the tropics or from tropical areas so weak and susceptible to diseases? There are basically two reasons:

1. The real wild caught fish are generally badly treated during their transport from their catching stations to the intermediary distributors or wholesalers. Diseases that appear are treated prophylactically, and without regard for how strong the medicine that is being used really is, as long as it cures the fish.

2. While demand is large, breeders are only interested in raising fish for sale fast, and in as great numbers as possible, and quick breeding of the available stock. At the same time breeders are looking for schemes to enhance the coloration of the fish, and questionable practices such as the addition of hormones and antibiotics are being used. The result is that the fish that arrive for sale are small, show all their colors, but are in fact severely harmed, and will not really survive for very long, increasing the amount of disappointment that Hobbyists experience.

In addition breeders always want to offer novelties, this is also the case

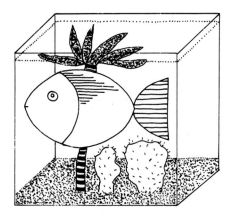

with plants, although many of these fish might not be suited for aquarium keeping. This could very well be fish which in nature grow up to a length of 3 or more feet. It is therefore understandable that such fish will give the Aquarist many problems. Such a fish is likely to attack and harass other aquarium inhabitants, and most likely will have aquatic plants on his daily menu.

Frequently fish that like to dig in the substrate are being sold. We can well imagine what the effects of such an addition are on a well planted aquarium. The only way to solve this problem is to remove the fish and try to rearrange the tank back to its original condition, and repair the damage done.

With plants such a mistake is obviously not as drastic as with fish. Because plants only »grow«, we can easily determine after a month or so, that either the plants grow too fast or do not grow at all.

The determination that these plants are not aquatic are then easy to make. Emers plants can be removed and replanted. The Aquarist should not be fooled and fall into the trap of attaching more importance to the fact that he wishes his plants inside the aquarium, and not on its side.

2.2.7.
Algae

After this digression, let us rather concentrate on Today's Aquarium, and in doing so we must obviously treat the subject of algae.

When an aquarium is set up too quickly, the Hobbyist will have to deal with a number of algae, this could be filamentous, beard and other algae. Other complications will also be common occurrances. Such problems are then attributed to not taking care properly of one's aquarium. Blue-green and filamentous algae cannot be overlooked, and they have to be dealt with immediately. Such action cannot be delayed even by a week. Indeed if one waits too long, for instance two weeks or more, it will practically be impossible to care with it at all.

In order to avoid the build up of algae right from the start, the aquarium should be run-in very slowly. Plants have to adjust themselves to the substrate, to the quality of the water, to the light, the temperature, the movement of the water and other such factors. When setting up his tank the hobbyist would do well to put algae-eating fish in the aquarium.

It does not make much sense of course to put 2 algae-eaters in a 400 liter aquarium (100 gallons), as those two fish would have to work »overtime« to keep up with the growth of algae. Here the aquarist should also know that algae-eaters work best in cleaning aquariums, when there are several of them instead of just one or two (a good comparison is a cleaning team in a building versus one cleaning lady having to do all the work). More about algae in Chapter 3.7.

1 Just about every hobbyist has at one time or another had to do with these algae. In the photo we show the green »Cladophora«-type algae. Green, hell green, in many shades of colour grow in larger and larger patches. In the end they cover entire parts of the aquarium.
2/3 (next page) Macro shots of the algae show that the long cells each contain many cell germs. Cladophora algae contain poison which results in the dying-off of higher forms of plant life. To be recommended for reading is the article by Dr. Eberhard Stengel in Aquarium Heute 1/84 and 3/84.

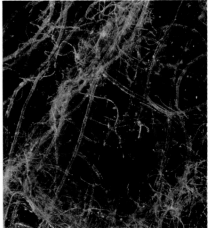
1

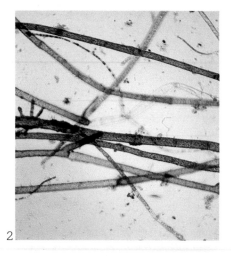

2

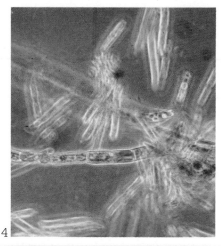

4

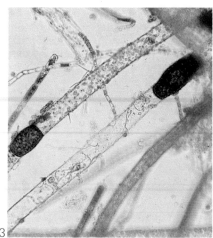

3

---

4 Enlarged view of a water drop from an aquarium. Next to a filamentous green algae, a large diatom and many small algae, especially Gyrosigma, can be seen.

It also seems that Aquarists are easily convinced to add anti algae products to their aquarium, and in doing so they become vulnerable to a number of other complications. This is certainly the wrong approach, especially during the initial period, when the aquarium is being run-in. It is as if all the plants were given a »knockout« right at the time when aquarium conditions should be at their optimum. Such practices obviously inhibit the growth, and make it much more difficult for plants to resist the appearance of algae on their leaves. A »chicken and egg« situation results, in which, by fighting the algae, the plants are being harmed; and since the plants are harmed they are no longer able to fight-off the growth of the algae. This process then continues without the aquarist having any chance to remedy the situation successfully. It is indeed impossible to produce an algae fighting product that can differentiate between algae and plants. The qualities of both are too close to each other.

2.2.8.
Light over the Aquarium

As important as oxygen is to the fish, light is to plants. Light indeed enables the photosynthesis process and the assimilation of nutrients by the plants in the aquarium, to take place.

When analyzing how aquariums are kept nowadays, we must over and over again come to the conclusion that lighting the aquarium is a subject that is still relatively unknown to the aquarist. Aquariums are still being placed in the immediate vicinity of natural light. This means, in practice, that when trying to determine the amount of light required by the tank we have to deal with an imponderable, namely the amount of natural light that falls on the tank everyday.

Nowadays, most aquariums are lit with fluorescent tubes. Unfortunately the types of lamps manufactured are not really designed with tank size and amount of light required by plants taken into consideration. In most cases lighting is far too low. Fluorescent tubes also give off heat, which raises the temperature of the water, because the lights are placed too close to the water. This can be particularly negative during the summer months. Overheating the aquarium for long periods of time is obviously not beneficial for fish and plant life.

Hobbyists can also take credit for discovering the utilization of special violet plant »growth promoting« lights, and adapting them for use above their aquariums. Unfortunately their increased utilization has brought with them a new set of problems. Worse even are the so-called black lights. They make plastic plants of all colors, sunken ships, skulls etc., stand out better, and show fish here and there, seemingly lost in the aquarium. Perhaps we should recommend that such Hobbyists not use live fish, but perhaps resort instead to using a few plastic or artificial ones.

In newly established aquariums the use of »plant growth« lamps undoubtedly, in our experience, promotes the growth of all kinds of undesirable slimey algae.

1 Aquarium with light hood. Danger of overheating in the summer.

Another mistake made in the lighting of the aquariums is the ever changing patterns and number of hours that the lights are left on. At certain times not enough light is provided, at others far too much. Many Aquarists switch the lights on and off several times during the day. A comparison to this is that we would be taking e.g. caffeine to go to sleep, and sleeping pills before going to work. This is perhaps a strong comparison, however a very close one to what Aquarists are doing. And on top, this is done at the most unexpected times. As a result one can certainly not expect any type of regular plant growth or any type of consistancy in what we observe when watching how plants are doing in such aquariums.

As said, aquarists do not take into account that lights that lie over the aquarium, close to the water, develop quite an amount of heat. This has two main drawbacks: 1. the amount of actual light given off by such lamp, is easily reduced by 50 % over a period of as short as 6 months. 2. the increase in water temperature resulting from the heat generated by these lamps, especially in the summer, pushes the temperature of the aquarium water above acceptable levels, with the resulting problems for fish and plants.

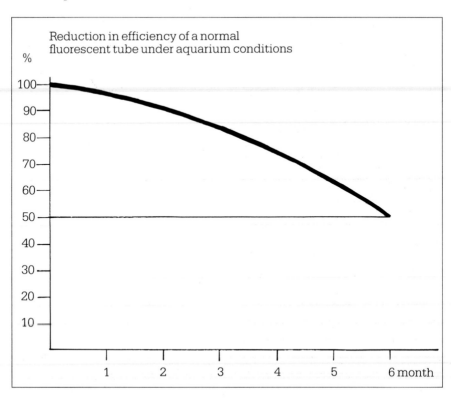

Reduction in efficiency of a normal fluorescent tube under aquarium conditions

2.2.9.
Heating

Let us now briefly deal with the last point, for the time being, in evaluating present day aquariums. Everyone obviously agrees that in a tropical fish aquarium the temperature of the water should be tropical. What tropical means is however subject to a great number of interpretations and conflicting suggestions. If this were not so, people would not be suggesting a certain number of watts per gallon of water in the aquarium. As a result of these recommendations the amount of watt that is being applied to the aquariums is much too high, and it is not being applied in a consistant and slow manner. This results in temperature fluctuations which have a definite negative influence on the fish and plants. In addition to this the effect of using strong heaters complicates matters further. Strong heaters stay on for shorter periods of time, than lower wattage heaters. More frequent on/off cycles result in a shorter heater life span. And this can of course lead to further complications, as we all know.

How the heating in an optimum aquarium should be applied is the subject of Chapter 3.10, and we will go in further detail on the subject there. Enough about our views for the time being.

Some Aquarists might be a little surprised that we are taking such a negative approach to the present day Tropical Fish Keeping practices. We do not do this because it gives us pleasure to point out the mistakes that are being made. We feel however that based on our observations, and what we have seen over the years while keeping tropical fish and plants ourselves, we can come forward and suggest a number of ways in which these practices can be improved. It is obvious that through experiments and observation one can arrive at better methods and make recommendations that will enable the Aquarist to see which methods are more desirable in the long run, especially if they lead to the Optimum Aquarium. Many will say that it is not easy to differentiate between a right and a wrong way. To that we say that today Tropical Fish Keeping has achieved a status that is of a much higher professional nature than it used to be in the past. Such a discipline is no longer a matter of luck, but a system in which results can be reproduced over and over again, so that we can speak of facts rather than assumptions. What has been happening in the Tropical Fish Keeping hobby in the last seven years is definitely a revolution. If this were not the case we would certainly not have come out with this handbook to the »Optimum Aquarium«.

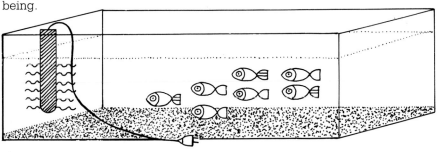

3.
The Optimum Aquarium

Enough has been said in our belief about Tropical Fish Keeping of yesterday and today. On one hand, there is definitely enough literature available that everyone can refer to, and on the other hand the critique we have brought out so far suffices to demonstrate our point, and it makes no sense to further lament about its shortcomings, since no one is really that interested.

What is of much more interest to us than the Tropical Fish Keeping of yesterday and today, is the Tropical Fish Keeping of tomorrow, as we are convinced that all Aquarists' intent is to keep an »Optimum Aquarium«. This will become more and more important in the Hobby as time goes on. From both the contents of this book and the positions that we have taken so far, it should be clear that all the subjects covered in this book will enable an Aquarist who follows our guidelines in the right sequence, to set up a tropical fresh water aquarium without any problems, and practice the keeping of the Optimum Aquarium without difficulty.

Before we outline and discuss the individual steps required to set up such an Optimum Aquarium however, we would like to lay down the ground rules. Notwithstanding all the imponderables arising from building an aquarium, the chemical diversity of the basic water and other components of the artificial biotope an aquarium is, nature's laws still underly the biological processes that take place. The results obtained will depend on how the Aquarist manages to control the chemical and physical reactions and processes that occur in the small amount of water that is contained in his aquarium. This needs to be recognized if the Aquarist wishes to maintain an aquarium in which life can be maintained and reproduced, and in which luck and chance do not intervene. In order to take this chance factor out of the keeping of ornamental and tropical fish and plants we

1 The open aquarium has re-entered our living-room. Modern hanging-type lights, which also bring greater security, have made this possible. Both HQL and HQI lights give strong light, down to the substrate.

have put together a number of rules that we feel are critical and unavoidable if one wishes to be successful in keeping an optimum aquarium.

We would like to introduce these 10 Golden Rules for the Optimum Aquarium in this book.

10 Golden Rules for the Optimum Aquarium

1. Tropical Warmth in the Substrate and in the Water

With: the Dupla 42 Volt Cable Heating System
Guarantees: a) Safety for hobbyist and fish
b) Enhanced and prolonged life of substrate used
c) Optimum nutrient and oxygen exchange

2. Aquarium-specific Lighting

With: the Dupla Lighting System
Guarantees: a) Good plant growth
b) Natural fish colouring
c) Optimum oxygen availability

3. Chemically stable Water

With: the Dupla CO_2 System
Guarantees: a) Neutral pH stabilisation
b) Optimum availability of CO_2
c) Stable carbonate hardness (Acid binding capacity)

4. Nature-like Plant Feeding

With: the Dupla Fertiliser System
Guarantees: a) Healthy plants
b) Continuous supply of nutrients
c) Tropical-type iron availability
d) Reduction of dissolved waste products as water is changed

5. Biological Filtration

With: the Dupla Bioball Trickle Filter or an oxygen-saving water circulation filter
Guarantees: a) Purer water
b) Nitrate reduction

6. Strong Water Movement

With: Circulation and Filter Pumps
Guarantees: a) Nutrient exchange between substrate, water and plants
b) Sufficient water movement for active fish
c) Uniform water quality and temperature within the aquarium

7. Dense Planting

With: pre-cultivated Aquarium Plants
Guarantees: a) Decorative overall impression
b) Good oxygen supply to gravel and water
c) Smooth running-in of aquarium
d) Algae prevention
e) Optimum water maintenance through regular breakdown of nitrogen compounds (e.g. nitrate)

8. Harmonious Fish Population

With: a correct choice of fish
Guarantees: a) Algae prevention by algae-eaters
b) No plant-eaters
c) Snail reduction by snail-eaters
d) A harmonious interplay of suitably matched fish

9. Tropical Fish Care

With: regular, partial water changes, and water treatment with Duplagan as well as easily digested fishfood with vitamins, and all necessary additives
Guarantees: a) Healthy and lively fish
b) Outstanding breeding results

10. Control of all Variables

With: the Dupla Diagnostic and Analysis System
Guarantees: a) Early recognition of potential problems
b) Timeliness of corrective measures
c) Avoidance of mistakes when setting up new aquariums

Copyright: Dupla Rescue mb GmbH

3.1.1.
Tropical Warmth in Substrate and Water

The important word in the above title is »and« between water and substrate. By using heating cable we are able to integrate the substrate completely into the aquarium. This is the result of the physical law that warm water rises from the substrate. In addition to having a uniform heat throughout the aquarium, we also achieve an exchange between the water and the substrate bringing the nutrients in the water and to the leaves and vice versa, the water that enters the substrate brings it the necessary oxygen. Since cold water has a tendency to sink, it draws oxygen in the substrate. This in turn helps in metabolizing organic materials, since as this water warms up and rises back to the surface it maintains a continuous beneficial exchange of nutrients and oxygen in the aquarium substrate and the water. No black anaerobic zones are created anywhere, which is a major advantage, as most of us know. With this system we are duplicating what is happening in nature, a horizontal and vertical exchange of both water and nutrients in a water mass.

3.1.2.
Aquarium-specific Lighting

For the lighting of the aquarium the Aquarist can resort to either fluorescent tubes, mercury vapor lamps, or metal halide high pressure lamps, depending on the size and type of aquarium. With such lights it is possible to show off the natural colors of the fish and obtain the kind of plant growth that is desired. What we are how ever also looking for in this respect is that during the day the aquarium water reaches an optimal oxygen content. This is in the neighbourhood of 100 % saturation. This is not only a requirement for the fish, but even more so a requirement for the tank as an eco-system, as a whole. Indeed not only fish require oxygen, but so do all the bacteria that are present in the aquarium and that are so necessary to metabolize and mineralise all the organic material from fish feeding and plants. Mineralization of these components or compounds is critical if we wish to maintain our aquarium under optimum conditions. In addition to that, close to 100 % saturation during the night, is necessary as plants require a good deal of oxygen, and if we did not obtain this through correct lighting, we would be facing possible catastrophic consequences.

3.1.3.
Chemically stable Water

For the chemical layman this is possibly difficult to understand, easily overlooked and not practiced.

Required are a neutral pH, stable acid buffering capacity and a carbonate hardness of at least 3° to 4° dH/1 dH = 17 ppm CaO. Why? In a community aquarium we maintain fish that come from acid waters, e.g. neon fish, as well as fish that come from alkaline waters, for instance perch. A neutral pH is therefore the ideal compromise if we want to maintain several species of fish in the community aquarium.

To obtain such a neutral pH we rely on the addition of carbon dioxide (CO_2) fertilization. However to be able to utilize CO_2 in the aquarium the water requires a carbonate hardness of at least 3° to 4° dH, because if it is lower, other acids could give the appearance CO_2 is present, simulate its presence so to speak, and show up in tests. On the other hand such carbonate hardness allows the required permanence and stability to be maintained (CO_2 content).

3.1.4.
Nature-like Plant Feeding

The chemical and as a result the nutrient content of many tropical waters is known.

Many are so poor in dissolved salts, that some of the necessary life-sustaining nutrients, especially the trace elements, are present only in very small amounts. The different nature of these waters however, e.g. running water because of its intensive contact with the substrate, or in other words the nutrient reservoir, ensures the constant re-supply of these substances. In addition many natural waters are different in their chemical structure. In an aquarium however, the supply of nutrients cannot be left to chance.

The basic nutrients, not present in tap water, are delivered at the same time as making regular water changes. At the same time regular water changes ensure that breakdown products of fish and plants are removed.

The chemically sensitive trace elements, such as iron, manganese, and many others, are added in small doses every day, as they cannot be added in large quantities e.g. once a week, because this might poison the aquarium.

3.1.5.

Biological Filtration

The task at hand is half completed if the Aquarist uses water circulation methods that save oxygen consumption, unfortunately experience shows that water is circulating for weeks on end over the same filter material, resulting in a filter bed that accumulates organic material, leaves and other pieces of plants, excess food and other such detritus. This is of course a method that greatly reduces oxygen and carries filtration on ad absurdum.

To solve this problem one has to either change the filter material regularly (e.g. filter wool), or use one of the now popular and long lasting »trickle« filters. The later greatly increase the amount of dissolved oxygen, and even reduce or control nitrate buildup, if properly run.

3.1.6.

Strong Water Movement

Good water movement is required to achieve an even water temperature throughout the Aquarium. It also ensures that organic breakdown material is washed away from the leaves on one hand, and new nutrients are brought to the leaves on the other. Especially broadleaved plants require strong water movement, to ensure that the waterfilm that otherwise build up because of adhesion forces, gets removed by the current created in the aquarium.

In addition, fish coming from running waters (brook or rivers) require a strong flow of water over their bodies (fish gymnastics).

3.1.7.

Dense Planting

The reason for planting mature plants right from the very start in the aquarium are as follows: Besides enhancing the aesthetic appearance of the aquarium, the root structure that plants develop continuously penetrates the substrate and supplies it with oxygen. It prevents blackening to the substrate. Optimal oxygen availability and algae prevention are thus facilitated. The plants do a great deal more for the aquarium however. It has been scientifically proven that well looked after plants remove noxious elements and certain disease causing elements from the water, thus contributing to the health of the fish. Certain plants even release very small amounts of antibiotic-like substances in the water, and thus improve the health of the fish.

3.1.8.

Harmonious Fish Population

This is understood as balancing the fish

species kept together, to eliminate aggressive behavior, especially in smaller aquariums. Territoriality can become a major cause for infighting when many different species are being kept together. It is also strongly recommended to include algae-eaters when selecting fish for one's aquarium. This could for instance be *Epalzeorhynchus siamensis*. And it is a good idea to include snail-eating fish, such as *Tetraodon palembangensis*.

3.1.9.
Tropical
Fish Care

This includes using the correct type of fish food and also making sure that the water is correctly prepared and/or adjusted before use. Tropical fish can be kept healthy and in good shape for extended periods of time, if the Aquarist uses a very high quality, vitamin-rich food. Since tropical fish come from waters that are often poor in dissolved salts, we need to point out that the food used should be poor in such salts, as otherwise difficult to cure intestinal problems might occur.

3.1.10.
Control
of all Variables

Through regular testing of aquarium conditions the Aquarist can prevent potential problems, by making sure that any changes occuring in the tank do not go unnoticed. This applies especially to the pH value fluctuations, nitrite content, but also to the amount of iron present in the water, the carbonate hardness, etc. Compared to nature, an aquarium contains such a small amount of water, it is like a puddle, small problems can rapidly deteriorate and have major consequences on the life in the tank, since they can go quickly from one extreme to the other. In an aquarium consistant conditions and consistant values are an absolute necessity.

Correct diagnosis and correct care are only »therapy« that will allow the aquarist to spot potential problems before they cause any upsets, and enable him to take corrective measures before any harm is done.

1 This photo, taken in a German Pet Shop, is proof that the professionals also embrace the idea of the Optimum Aquarium.

1

3.2
The Aquarium

Now that we have identified the constraints that we have to deal with if we want to keep a well running Optimum Aquarium, we can start concentrating on the individual building blocks, and make recommendation for each of them.

At the basis of the hobby is the aquarium, or as some Aquarists call it the »tank«. We will use both of these names.

Once one decides to start up an aquarium, one has no problems in selecting a model, since that task has become quite easy. A wide choice of all-glass aquariums, or aluminum framed, built with inert silicone glues, are available in many shapes and sizes. They are now also much lighter and longer lasting.

All such aquariums can also be used for salt water. This is only of interest to the freshwater aquarist if he has to deal with very soft water. Infrequently aquariums made in the old fashioned way, with Eternit, are to be found, but they are no longer being manufactured.

One should never try to save when buying an aquarium, as quality will suffer, and those small savings might transpire into great expenses, should the tank at a later date leak or break, or be inadequate in some other fashion. An aquarium of good quality should last forever.

When buying, we need to look at the way the aquarium is finished: whether e.g. the glass is polished and the silicone seals are clean and well finished. The quality of the seals is important to prevent algae from growing between the glass and the silicone, as such algae are extremely hard to remove. In this respect gray and black silicone are particularly good as they reduce algae growth in the seams because they do not let light through. Just about all aquariums sold today are no longer reinforced, and the aluminium or plastic frames only serve a decorative purpose, and assist when putting the aquarium together at the manufacturing stage. They do not contribute to the strength of the aquarium.

Working with glass has now progressed to the point that it has become possible to build tanks of any shape or size. Even holes can be drilled in the sides or the bottom, if desired, to set up filtration or water return, in a more aesthetic way. One can now order such tanks from many pet stores. Additionally one can acquire connectors made out of inert PVC, e.g. elbows, tees, bulkhead fittings, ball valves, etc. from plumbing supply places. This allows for a much more professional looking set up, and is easy to install using the special bonding agents that are sold at the same places.

3.2.1.
Measurements

When selecting an aquarium one should not only look at the traditionally rectangular shapes which nicely fit on the top of cabinets, but one should also demonstrate some sense of daring and use novel shapes which are now being offered in tropical fish stores. Unfortunately the standard tanks that one can find are usually still too narrow and too tall. Wider aquariums are much easier to decorate. One should also consider the fact that higher aquariums are more expensive because thicker glass has to be used when they are built, this because of the high pressure at the bottom of the tank. We can however see a trend developping where Aquarists are buying wider aquariums of the so-called »Dutch« type. Before buying an aquarium one should of course take into consideration that the available measurements are usually built around the normalized length of fluorescent tubes available on the market. There are fluorescent tubes of non-standard measures, however they are more expensive. (The lumilux tubes, which deliver 30 % more light than other fluoescent tubes, are only available in standard lengths.) The following measurements are standardized at the production stage: 60 cm 20 watts, 90 cm 30 watts, 120 cm 40 watts, 150 cm 65 watts.

Since we can of course not place a 60 cm fluorescent tube over a 60 cm aquarium, the length of the aquarium should be at least 10 cm more than the length of the tube. So when using fluorescent tubes, the ideal measurement of the aquarium would be either 70 cm, 100 cm, 130 cm or 160 cm.

When giving aquarium measurements, very frequently the depth, the height and the width are easily confused. In order to avoid confusion we would like to introduce the following concept that will hopefully avoid any further confusion. We define the three measurements of the aquarium by the letters a, b and c. a and b represent the length of the aquarium and the width of the aquarium when measured on the bottom glass panel, (the base). c is then the height of the aquarium.

The ideal measurements for an optimum aquarium would therefore for instance be: 70 × 45 × 35 cm or 100 × 50 × 40 cm or 130 × 60 × 45 cm or 160 × 65 × 50 cm.

The calculation of the content is then as follows: a × b × c divided by 1000. (In U.S. gallons a × b × c in inches divided by 231).

For instance: $\dfrac{160 \times 65 \times 50}{1000} = 520$ liter.

We all know that 1 liter of water weighs 1 kilo. It follows that the water contained in the above aquarium weighs 520 kilo. Based on experience we have to add another 20 % to account for decoration (gravel, stones) and installation of filters etc., or in this case an extra 110 kg.

This works out to a total of 630 kg. And this does not include the weight of the stand.

---

1 This photo demonstrates the modern sized aquarium (left) as opposed to the one commonly used. Modern aquariums offer more decoration possibilities and give at the same time the possibility to have light penetrate to the substrate level.

1

In many houses the allowable weight per square meter is however only 150 kg.

When installing large aquariums, a discussion with the architect who designed the house, might therefore be prudent. In addition the allowed weight is less in the middle of a room, as less support exists there. It is therefore better to place the aquarium along a wall.

The aquarium should also be installed in such a way that enough space is available for hanging lights over it. In addition there should be at least 15 cm between the water surface and the bottom of the light to allow space for taking care of the aquarium.

3.2.2.
Where to place the Aquarium

It is recommended to place the aquarium in such a way so that it receives no, or as little as possible, daylight. Indeed the amount of daylight is hard to control and cannot be quantified. Because of the types of lighting that are available on the market nowadays, we are no longer dependent on daylight when running our aquariums.

The height of the stand should be such that the aquarium can easily be looked into when sitting down (it should be at eye level).

Trunk chests or stands can be used, and they are nowadays available in many colors. They all have sufficient space to house the filters and other items we are using while caring for our fish and plants.

We need to ensure that it is absolutely level by using a carpenters level. Adjustments can easily be made if necessary. You will be surprised to find how many floors are uneven, and you can therefore not assume they are, but have to verify. This needs obviously to be done before the tank is being filled with water. Between the aquarium and the stand use a soft, compressable material, such as foam or styrofoam, to absorb vibrations caused by trucks, cars, etc. in the street. This will also reduce stress on the glass, from any uneveness that might still exist. It also acts as a thermal barrier for the bottom of the aquarium.

Also make sure that electric outlets are within easy reach to allow for easy connection of instruments you are using. Ideally a water source, an even better a drain, should be nearby.

3.2.3.
Miscellaneous

Once the aquarium is positioned and one starts considering the possibilities that exist for the location of all the other instruments that one is using, it is important to remember that holes have to be made to allow for the various cables that connect the sensors, probes, etc. to the actual devices.

This can typically be filter type or hose, light cable, a heating cable and wire as well as regulating cable, feeding device pH electrode cable, carbon dioxide hose, as well as for the dosing of nutrients. As can be seen quite a few provisions need to be made before the tank is set up for these wires to run in and out of the tank into the stand either through its top plate, side or back.

Planning their exact location in advance will save a lot of effort and aggravation afterwards.

It might be helpful to string all these cables together and run them through one piece of pipe or hose for neatness.

Taking these precautions will simplify the aquarists life a great deal later on. Inside the cabinet or stand all the instruments and control devices can be mounted on a board so that it is easy to access them and switch them on and off as required. It might also be advisable to include a timing

1 Electrical switchboard with timers and pilot lights.
2 Modern aquarium with overflow corner box built-in
3 Example of arrangement of control and protection instruments and heating device. Installed on special board. From left to right: CO_2 bottle, with pressure reducer. PH continuous controller, temperature continuous controller, dosing pump for fluids and liquid fertiliser. Bottom: 42 Volt transformer.

1

2

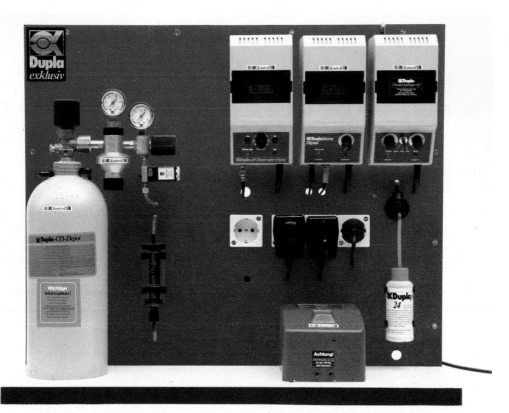

3

device that regulates the number of hours that the fish and plants receive light.

The cabinet underneath should of course be large enough to house devices such as the CO_2 container, the regulator and also the electronic pH meter, the heating regulating device and also the pump dispensing fertilizer or other liquids in the tank. All the important test kits, liquid fertilizer as well as the diagnostic checklist and the aquarist's diary containing all the tank conditions, can also be kept in that chest. Various kinds of food, and fertilizer for the plants, kept in the same area will make it easier for the aquarist to maintain his tank in good conditions, as experience proves that easy access to everything that is required while maintaining one's tank definitely improves the degree of care that is being dispensed. Of course if additional space is still available perhaps other items such as replacement floss and nets and glass cleaners can also be kept there.

The tank described so far is now ideal both from the standpoint of its size, its execution, the place it occupies in the room and all the technical equipment as well as miscellaneous items required that are being used. This also completes the discussion on the first and important building block in setting up an optimum aquarium.

3.3.
The Substrate

Now that our aquarium has been installed and is in the place where we want it, we can start putting in the substrate. As with many other things that have to do with Tropical Fish Keeping one can easily find many and sometimes contradictory recommendations as to what one should do than what one should not do.

3.3.1.
Differences of Opinion

Discussions about the right kind of substrate for an aquarium have been going on

for as long as Tropical Fish Keeping has been in existance. There are two conflicting main lines of thought. Some contend that the plants take up the nutrients they require through the roots, and therefore they require a substrate rich in fertilizer and such nutrients. To make sure that the plants really are not missing anything some of these experts even recommend to add substances such as cow dung or rabbit droppings. Others are of the opinion that the roots only serve to maintain the plant in a fixed position in the ground, and that plants receive their nutrients through the leaves and take it directly out of the water. For such people of course a substrate should only consist out of clean sand and gravel.

Great minds cannot agree on what the substrate should be! Lengthy discussion ensure as well as a multitude of recipes, some widely publicized and others kept as if they were the most precious and greatest secrets. Receiving such secret tips is of course nothing new and indeed some of them can work for a short period of time but we certainly do not recommend that aquarists try to duplicate them when setting up an optimum aquarium. If the advocates of »rich« or »poor« substrate were on the right track, experience should have given us the winner a long time ago. This did however not occur.

In the meantime it has been proven through many experiments that the composition of the substrate has a definite and great influence on the growth and general state of aquatic plants. As a result we can no longer accept the notion that the substrate only serves the plants as a hold fast.

3.3.2.
The Substrate: Your Aquarium's Chemical Factory

It is a fact that the substrate has several important tasks to accomplish for plants to grow in the proper way, and also that many extremely complicated biochemical processes take place in that substrate.

One of its most important tasks consists

in providing the plants with fertilizer in a manner that the plants can absorb. When dealing with the chapter »water« (Chapter 3.4) we will demonstrate again that oxygen in the water oxidizes a lot of the fertilizer available and chemically transforms it in compounds that are not absorbable by the plants, or combines certain chemicals in a manner not suitable for the plants. These chemicals that are so important for plants are amongst others iron, manganese, nitrogen and a number of trace elements. In the chemical factory that the substrate is, the processes that take place because of the lesser amount of oxygen available, are of the reduction type and as a result the nutrients made available are suitable for absorption by the plants the nutrients and thus make them. This means that rather than bound or precipitated, these nutrients are now back in solution and can easily be absorbed.

In addition it is of course also important that the now reduced nutrients be released from the substrate so that they are available to the leaves of the plants, and can serve as additional fertilization by being generally distributed in the water of the aquarium.

Under gravel filtration, as is very frequently recommended today disturbs the substrate too much, and pulls too much oxygen in it. Much better are the results obtained by low voltage cable heating, which will be further discussed in this chapter.

As a result of heating the substrate and because of the fact that warm water has a tendency to rise, we are in fact creating a slight amount of circulation from the substrate into the main water mass of the aquarium. Which is important just from the point of use alone that it mitigates the chemical processes taking place there. Should this not occur, the substrate will turn black, and start decaying.

There are of course a number of other methods recommended to get this kind of movement in the substrate, starting with using much larger type of gravel, to using any of the multitude of under gravel filters that are on the market. We feel however that none of these are to be recommended for the reasons already explained. Since our goal is to maintain an Optimum Aquarium, it is however important that we resolve the problem of substrate throughflow in an efficient way, since only then will the chemical factory that the substrate is function properly.

---

1 The picture on page 51 shows the water flow sources in natural waters. Both vertical and horizontal water movement ensures that few anaerobic areas exist, and that no areas turn black, as can often be the case in an aquarium.

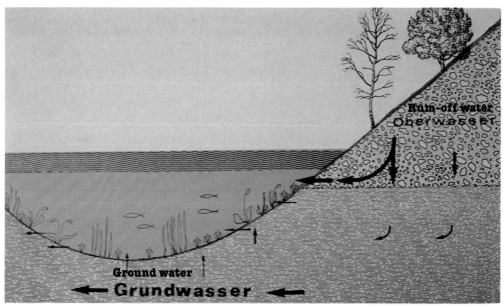

3.3.3.
Nature as an Example

How should the substrate be to obtain the results that we have described above? Let us look at the habitat where most of our aquarium plants are coming from and growing in.

Typical for the water in which these plants grow (about which we have more to say in Chapter 3.4. and 3.6.) is that the presence of iron in both the substrate and the actual water mass. Characteristic thereof is the red brownish color of the substrate and of the river banks.

At this stage we would like to interject, while it is appropriate, a remark about the pioneer time of Tropical Fish Keeping. Let us remind you of the many success stories we all have heard about aquariums with rusty bottoms in which plants were doing

1

marvelously well. And who does not know about the famous rusty nail lying on the bottom of the tank? It is amazing how certain Aquarists have, in thos early days, pinpointed exactly what needed to be done to ensure better plant growth without knowing what was happening in the tropics. In their natural habitat plants will grow in many kinds of soil including gravel, clay substrate as well as in substrate that is slimy and full of branches, leaves, twigs other kinds of foliage and even slough. Between those two there is obviously a considerable difference and that is the reason that it is not easy to recommend a particular type of substrate that is ideal. Once in a while one can also find plants that grow well in ground that is tough, interspersed with a network of roots, branches, to the point where it is practically impossible to take the plants out without damaging them. This can then only be achieved using a number of tools such as a shovel etc.

What was however a common point at all the sites investigated and substrates analyzed, was that the ground always showed a consistant and continuous through flow of water brought about by strong bottom circulation.

No signs of darkened substrate were observed in any of the plant regions.

Unfortunately the situation is entirely different in an aquarium. Because of its design it is normal that water in an aquarium has a tendency to stagnate. As a result this water can very quickly become low in dissolved oxygen content, with the resulting anaerobic acitvity, and the substrate turning black. This will also result in the slow but sure dieing off of all plants, as a substrate that is so poor in oxygen cannot sustain for even brief periods of time the growth of any plants. The only thing that can be done in such a case is to take the tank apart and start all over again, as such a substrate cannot be saved.

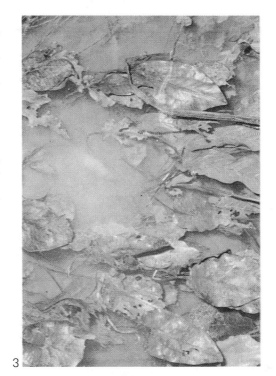

3

---

1 Typical laterite area in the tropics.
2 In this Crypotocoryne area in South Thailand we removed the in photo 3 shown substrate. Analysis demonstrated a high iron content. Unlike often in the aquarium, the roots of the cryptocoryne were not white but brown (next page).

4

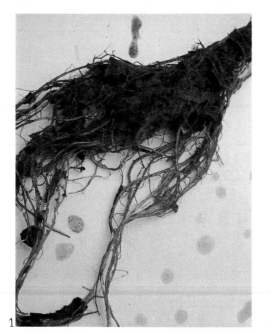

1 The brown color of the roots of the
Cryptocoryne cordata changes. It is due to
the iron sludge which can be removed.
2 That the substrate has a large influence
on plant growth is shown in this example:
3 C. wendtii in iron containing gravel,
4 Gravel turf substrate (both cultured
submers).

3.3.4.
Substrate: A Two Way Solution

For a really optimum substrate a solution is
available which consists of two basic components: the first one is heating the substrate by means of a low voltage heating
cable, and the second one the addition of a
supplement to the substrate, which acts
like laterite in tropical waters.

Many of you will of course ask what is laterite and what role does it play in the substrate?

Laterite is a red type of earth that is
primarily found in the tropics. Anyone having traveled in the tropics both in Africa
and Asia will certainly have noticed how
frequently the earth is red, and how commonly this fact is noticeable throughout all
these regions.

It is mainly for climatological reasons
that laterite is only found in the tropics. Laterite consists of beside kaolin (terra alba)
a great deal of ferric oxide and ferric hy-
droxide (from 4 to 84 percent). While there is
no use for laterite in agriculture, it does play
a significant role in water cultures and also
for submersed growing of plants. Iron is released under anaerobic conditions in
ground water due to the action of organic
acids and humic acids. The same occurs in

streams. Brown to rust-brown leaching, and oozing, from such substrates can easily be observed. We have named these leachings »nutrient springs« as they contain just about every nutrient that can under normal conditions only dissolve with great difficulty in water, and only as trace elements. (See also 3.4.6.)

In large open waters the following normally takes place: with the presence of oxygen, iron and non-organic trace elements are oxidized and precipitated. A red brown sediment forms and deposits itself on the substrate. Many aquatic plants show signs on their leaves of the precipitation of these »iron clouds«. This is in fact what gives tropical waters their typical color.

Down to the deep layers of the soil of tropical waters these deposits of iron can be found. Depending on the organic or the content in organic acids and humic acids of these various waters certain quantities of iron are dissolved and released in the water.

The addition of iron rich additives has the same function in an aquarium. Under slightly anaerobic conditions in the aquarium substrate and also thanks to the activity of plant roots tiny amounts of iron are dissolved and go back in solution. (This occurs under the effect of organic acids released by the plants themselves). The iron containing additive is mixed with the ac-

tual substrate used in a ratio of approximately 1 to 3 before it is placed in the aquarium, and the mix thus prepared makes up the bottom layer of the substrate. This is then covered up with the balance of the substrate that you have selected (e.g. gravel) once this is completed the water can then be added to the aquarium, however paying close attention not to disturb the substrate too much.

The combination of low voltage heating cable and the laterite which you have added to the tank make up a very important link in insuring that the aquarium runs properly. Indeed because of the physical laws described earlier the uniform heat that is generated by this heating cable results in a small but continuous water movement between the substrate and the actual aquarium water mass, and in essence a water circulation system has now been established using the principle that warm water rises and cold water sinks. The colder

1 Pure laterite substrate (Duplarit) in granule form. The iron content of laterite differs. For aquariums a high content is needed.
2 We recommend this quartz gravel (2–3 mm) of which the bottom third is mixed with laterite (Duplarit).

1 Mixing laterite with gravel is best done in a bucket.
2 This mixture is used to cover the bottom of the aquarium before the heating cable was installed. Wetting the bottom glass plate makes it easier to string the heating cable.
3 Finally the 2/3 remaining gravel is put in the aquarium, after washing it. Then the water can be added carefully.

water in turn now enters the substrate replaces the warmer water that has just escaped from it and is in turn heated up and rises back into the tank. The substrate is now an integral part of the aquarium.

All other efforts to obtain similar results using other devices have failed in achieving the kind of nutrient circulation that we have described in this chapter. Many of these devices either function much too quickly and do not allow for chemical processes to take place, or they function in such a way that the water circulation is not uniform at all. Indeed water always tries to find the way of least resistance and what we have just stated can easily be demonstrated by using coloring agents and dyes, to trace how the water exactly flows through the gravel. That the circulation is not uniform is obvious and as a result the effect of the through-flow has been partially lost, indeed it does not keep the substrate cum chemical factory working.

3.3.5.
Substrate Testing

Before we close this chapter we would like to make a very important recommendation. Regardless of whether a special mixture, or gravel is being used for the aquarium substrate, before using it it should be tested to make sure that it does not contain lime. Indeed a substrate containing lime, would result in rising carbonate hardness, once we add CO_2 to the water, and would counter-act our attempts to bring the water in lime-carbonic acid balance. As the carbonate hardness keeps rising, more and more free CO_2 is required, to keep the pH at a neutral level. A detailed explanation on tests to be done on the substrate can be found under the heading decoration in Chapter 3.11.2.

3

3.4.
The Water
3.4.1.
The Water
in the Tropical Brook

Many readers will probably be surprised that after everything we have already said about water, that we are devoting another chapter to this subject. We feel however that water is such an important constituent of our aquarium that not enough can be said about it.

We already pointed out that whoever has explored a tropical brook or river, will have noticed great differences between such streams and the ones that we commonly find in our own backyards. Over and over-again we see the red-brown substrates and the ocre colored deposits of ferric hy-droxide on the river banks. One can also see in certain streams clouds of apparently de-caying material, moving through the water, which deposits itself in thick layers on the plants and their leaves. When analyz-ing this material it turns out that it does have a very high iron content. The water in those streams also contains a much higher amount of dissolved iron than we would normally find in our own streams, brooks and rivers.

This should come as no surprise when we look at the geology of tropical regions. The high iron content of the waters has its origin in the laterite rich soil over which these streams flow (we have discused this

1 This photo demonstrates a typical phenomenon of tropical waters. The iron entering the water, in solution, at the leaching areas, is oxydised and precipi-tates. It floculates, sinks and falls on the leaves and substrate. In the picture on leaves of Barclaya longifolia. Result: a sediment high in iron builds up.

1

in detail in Chapter 3.3.). From this sail aggressive ground water dissolves the iron and mixes it with the water of the stream.

This should illustrate the importance of iron as a major component of the nutrients that the plants require. The yellowing and glassy appearance that certain plants get at certain periods, indicates that the iron content of the water is much too low (iron clorosis).

1

Portrait of a Cryptocorynes stream

1 The stream is only 1 km long and already Cryptocorynes are appearing.

2 Only a few 100 metres further the stream shows its nicest plant growth: Thousands of Cryptocoryne cordata.
3 Now other plants also appear: Crinum thaianum and Ceratophyllum demersum, and overgrow the Cryptocorynes.
4 And 800 metres further down the end of the stream C. ciliata indicates that the sea is not far away.

2

3

4

3.4.2.
Natural Water Movement

Let us look for a minute at a very obvious fact. Many of the aquatic plants that we use in our aquariums are, in their natural habitat, found in brooks that frequently are not much longer than 10 km (6.5 miles) but it is very noticeable that the water is running quite rapidly. Although these brooks are very short, they harbor quite a dense vegetation.

Even after a few 100 meters from the beginning of the brook, plant growth is very noticeable, for instance *Barclaya longifolia*, *Cryptocorynes*, *Crinum thaianum*, *ceratophillum* and other plants. Once in a while one can find entire areas where just one type of plant grows, at other times we find a substantial number of different plants mixed in one area. The growth is often so dense that the brook is threatened with silting up. As we near the end of the brook we find lots of *Cryptocorynes ciliata*, followed by Mangroves, which indicate that we are approaching a lake.

The speed of the water in these brooks is considerable, and has been measured at 3.5 meters per second, and frequently more. For our purpose this should indicate that when we keep these plants in the aquarium, especially those with long leaves such as *Cryptocorynes, Echinodorus, Vallisneria,* that we need to have a constant and strong water movement. This ensures that we supply the plants and their leaves with fresh water containing the numerous nutrients they require, and at the leaf surface. At the same time strong water movement will wash away any excretions from the plants, and prevent a thin water film from forming at the leaf surface, (adhesion forces).

---

1 Typical Biotope of a still water body: a so-called »tank« in Sri Lanka. Here a lot of plants well known to the Hobbyist grow, however no Cryptocorynes.

1

3.4.3.
Plants from Still Waters

An aquarium is, regardless of how much we make the water move, and how much we irate it, a mass of still water when we compare it with the natural habitats of the plants that we keep in it. Even regular weekly or biweekly water changes does not make an aquarium a running water like brook. A number of organic breakdown materials such as nitrates and other organic compounds will over time build up in the aquarium and are not used to such high concentration of these elements.

On the other hand we can also find a number of plants that do very well in aquariums especially those that in their own biotope come from still waters. An example of these plants are the so called »tanks« from Sri Lanca. These are pools and lakes which for the major part have been built artificially and which cover practically the entire country. The origin of these tanks goes back many many centuries, in fact before our time. Although the word might not sound very nice to us, it does bear a resemblance to the word we use ourselves such as tank and aquarium. These tanks contain many marsh and other water plants which can be easily kept in aquariums. Here, amongst each other grow plants such as *Hydrilla verticillata*, *Aponogeton*, *Utricularia*, *Myriophyllum*, *Bacopa*, *Rotata*, *Limnopholia*, but also *Ottelia alismoides*, *Ceratopteris thalictrides*, *Trapa maximowiczii*, *Limnocharis flava*, *Elodea* and *Sagittaria*. And of course very conspicuous are plants such as *Nymphoides christata*, *N. indica*, *Nymphaea stellata* and many, many others. Many of these »tanks« dry out during the dry season, but are filled with plants the next year when the rainy season returns.

3.4.4.
pH Value and Carbon Dioxide

In our attempts to determine the requirements for good growth of tropical plants in brook and stream water various substrates were analysised both chemically and physically. Part of these analyses were done on the spot during our expeditions. More complicated tests for which more technical equipment was required were done in our own laboratories. To do so we utilized hundreds of samples that we had carefully packed and brought back with us to Germany. When analyzing the pH values of these waters we encountered not only acidic but also alkaline and neutral waters (acidic pH below 7, alkaline above 7, neutral pH equal to 7). The streams in Thailand which had profuse growths of plants all showed pH values of between 5.7 and 6.2, or on the acidic side. Some of these streams showed a pH of approximately 1 unit higher and varied between 6.6 and 7.9. These variations stem from the fact that we are dealing with different geological formations. Water in regions with high calcarious deposits reacted in alkaline ways (Phangnga South Thailand). In these areas pH values of 8 were not uncommon because of the very high carbonate content of the water. The search for cryptocorynes was fruitless, however, we did find plants such as *Ottelia alismoides*, *Ceratopteris thalictroides* and others.

Our many analyses have demonstrated that the pH is very much dependent on the carbonate hardness of the water, the content of free carbon dioxide and also the humic and other organic acids present in the water.

Both carbon dioxide and humic acids performs very important tasks in the fertilizing of the water for our plants. Carbon dioxide is the supplier of the free carbon that our water plants so much require.

---

1 + 2 Part of the tests were done on site. For more detailed analysis, water samples were taken, some already in vials. Water was tested not only for macro nutrients, but also for trace elements.

Humic acids act as the carriers for a whole number of nutrients and trace elements that plants need such as iron, manganese, copper, zinc a. o. Without these organic substances they would only be present in the water in chemical combinations that plants cannot absorb and their presence would therefore be of no use to our aquatic plants.

3.4.5.
Softened Water poor in Salts

What is continuously fascinating and surprising how poor in dissolved salts and extremely soft the water from most tropical brooks was. One could compare it to slightly polluted distilled water. This would easily lead one to believe that this water would be poor in nutrients. The rich and diversified plant growth however seemed to prove the contrary. As not only were there numbers of species that were growing but also the quantities of each. The various tests proved once more that no lack of nutrients existed in these waters. Not one. The whole range of trace elements necessary for the growth and survival of the plants was complete. For a long time this was a

problem that we found very hard to solve. Even from a pure mathematical standpoint one would expect that with such quantities and diversification of species present that at least one nutrient would be lacking or would be under represented. This was not the case and we even discovered at our various measurement points, that further down the brook the concentrations of nutrients were even higher than at the locations where we had initially made our measurements. We found this very hard to explain and set out to discover the mysterious source of this unexplained availability of nutrients and fertilizer.

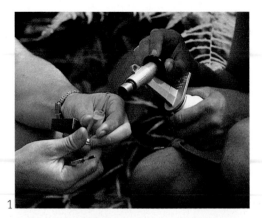

1

2

3.4.6.
Nutrients Supply through Nutrient Springs

After much research and many mistakes, one day we were lucky, and were able to observe what turned out to be the answer to our question. We witnessed red brown leachings close to one of the river banks. With great care we managed to make a quick analysis on the spot. We discovered that it contained large amounts of iron and manganese, and suddenly the answer to our questions was crystal clear. We had discovered the tropical stream nutrient supply. What was leaching in the tropical streams was the purest concentrate of fertilizer that could possibly be made.

More complete analyses was done in the lab later which confirmed our suspicions. The leachings contained 40 times more iron, 27 times more manganese, 20 time more nitrogen and 8 times more carbon than the water in the streams itself. The very special effect of these nutrient rich springs, resides in the fact that they contain mostly those nutrients that oxidize very easily and which disappears from the water in a very short period of time. These nutrient springs however seem to be active day and night during the dry and rainy seasons.

Having discovered them, we knew what to look for, and was able to spot them in just about every stream that we targeted, including rice fields along the banks of these rivers and streams. We now had proof that tropical brooks received permanent fertilization and that their waters contained more than adequate amounts of fertilizer all year round.

We also discovered that although the amount of water varies considerably at different times of the year (high water from the resulting floods, dry season during which the rivers turn into small streams) had in fact little effect on the chemical composition of the waters that we have been analyzing. An example hereof can be found in the results of analyses of water at 3 different times of the year, made in Southern Thailand, see page 66.

For the keeping of tropical fish this is obviously a very important discovery. It makes our task of providing the aquatic plants that we wish to maintain a lot simpler. The results are particularly interesting with regard to the raising of cryptocorynes as it had been advocated that the changes that occur during the year could be attributed to the changes in chemical composition of the water. It would now appear that only the physical effect of the high and low waters influence the manner in which a cryptocorynes develop, and whether they

1

2

flower or not. This was confirmed in 1975 when the rainy season did not arrive and that an unexpected low water period came about, as a result cryptocorynes responded by flowering although this was not the normal time of the year and although normally cryptocorynes can only flower up to a certain water level or above a certain water level.

1 We discovered the »nutrient springs« in tropical streams were nutrient rich water permanently leaches in the stream. The opalising effect of these leachings can be seen in the photo.
2 Even in the rice fields nutrient rich water is leaching in the bordering stream.
3 Inflorescence of Cryptocoryne cordata in a South Thailand stream. Especially during the dry season when water is low, Cryptocorynes flower profusely.

3

Nutrient springs at tropical brooks

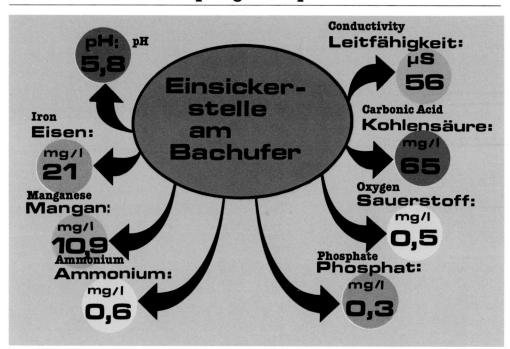

Comparison of analysis of stream water in Lam Kaen:				
		High water	Low water	Normal
Temp.	°C	W: 25, L: 31	W: 26, L: 29	W: 26, L: 30
LF	μS-cm[1]	25/21	27/23	26/22
GH	°dH	0.156	0.08	0.17
SBK		0.11	0.15	0.15
pH-value		6.3	5.6	5.5
RP	mV	260	235	245
RP	rH-W	29.5	27.4	27.6
CO_2	mg/l	8.25	14.3	13.5
O_2	mg/l	6.0	5.5	6.0
Ca	mg/l	0.8	0.6	0.69
Mg	mg/l	0.3	0.23	0.3
K	mg/l	1.62	1.35	1.65
Na	mg/l	2.50	3.30	2.60
HCO_3	mg/l	6.71	9.27	9.15
SO_4	mg/l	0.6	0.27	1.15
Cl	mg/l	2.62	4.5	8.0
PO_4	mg/l	0.307	0.056	0.648
NO_3	mg/l	5.6	–	0.47
NH_4	mg/l	0.05	0.06	0.02
Fe^2	mg/l	0.094	–	0.1
Fe^3	mg/l	0.068	–	0.02
Fe 2 + 3	mg/l	0.162	0.29	0.12
rel. F.	%	82 % 25 g/m³	90 % 26 g/m³	92 % 28 g/m³

1 We analysed various streams at different times of the year. Here a stream in South Thailand during the rainy season. The stream shows high-water.

2 The same Cryptocoryne stream during the dry season. The accumulating debris and leaves, will be washed away during the rainy season. Analysis also demonstrated very little change in the chemical composition of the water.

3.4.7.
Natural and Artificial Habitats

The complete water analyses we made brought other facts to light, tropical brooks are very balanced in their composition especially since the amount of nutrients available is evenly distributed and multifaceted. Certainly much more so than for instance mains water.

For instance, in mains water, calcium and magnesium make, on the average, up to 80 % of the hardness factors, in tropical waters only 50 %.

Potassium a very important nutrient is however not to be found in mains water. In some areas it is very limited, perhaps 3 %. In the tropics however potassium represents 17 % on average.

Also in the anion analysis large differences between mains and tropical water can be found (see p. 68 diagram).

It is, a result, without a doubt necessary to take these chemical differences into account, if one wishes optimum plant growth.

The plants which grow in our aquaria, do not only grow in Asia, but in many different countries and continents.

It is therefore, for the keeping of such plants, important to know these differences between natural and artificial water chemistries.

As a result we analysed, besides typical waters in Thailand, also water from Sri Lanka (Ceylon) and discovered certain water chemistry differences.

One can, besides the already indicated pH difference of one unity and the higher lime content of Ceylon water, also find a difference in the actual proportions of other nutrients.

The water from Ceylon comes much closer in its make-up, to the German water, than the one from Thailand.

This would explain to us why Cryptocorynes from Ceylon are easier to keep as other ones.

Here we see that the nutrient make-up has both cell growth and physiological impact on the plants.

Our research brought a number of important facts to light which are important for growing aquarium plants. These facts lead to the unavoidable, and great problem which results from the difference between a natural biotope and our home aquarium.

The consequences of these research results in both biotopes and in our labs were instrumental in bringing out the 10 golden rules for the keeping of the Optimum Aquarium.

In the chapters that follow, we will go into further detail on each of these problems mentioned above.

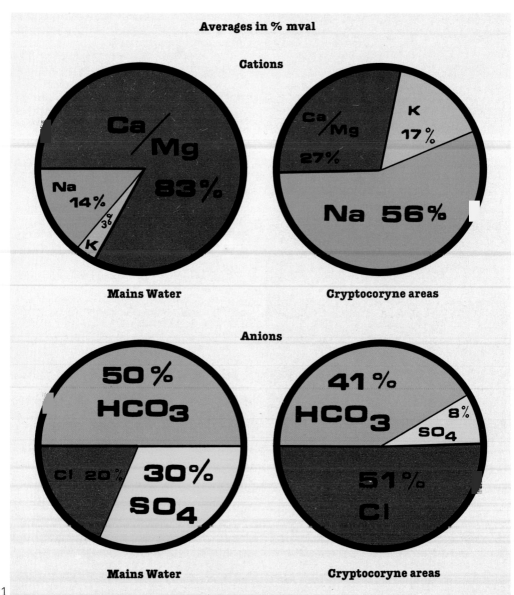

Averages in % mval

Cations

Ca/Mg 83%
Na 14%
K 3%

Mains Water

Ca/Mg 27%
K 17%
Na 56%

Cryptocoryne areas

Anions

50% HCO₃
Cl 20%
30% SO₄

Mains Water

41% HCO₃
8% SO₄
51% Cl

Cryptocoryne areas

Sequence of nutrients

Thailand	Ceylon	Mains water
Cations		
1. Sodium	Calcium	Calcium
2. Potassium	Sodium	Magnesium
3. Calcium	Magnesium	Sodium
4. Magnesium	Potassium	Potassium
Anions		
1. Chlorides	Bicarbonates	Bicarbonates
2. Bicarbonates	Chlorides	Sulphates
3. Sulphates	Sulphates	Chlorides

1 The picture on the other page demonstrates the difference between our mains water and water from a stream in South Thailand plant area. In mains water iron 2 is to be found, in tropical waters mostly iron 1 (cations). This is also demonstrated in the anion analysis. A listing of the most important ions is found above.

2 Typical Cryptocoryne biotope.

3.4.7.1.
Water in the Aquarium

Our study of the native waters in which aquarium plants grow has given us some important clues to the composition of good aquarium water.

A comparison of these analyses with our tap water shows that, whether hard or soft, it is far from ideal. We will proceed from the following position:

● The nutrient ratio in tap water is very unfavorable to plant growth,

● Several important plant nutrients are not contained from tap water.

The nutrient gap becomes more pronounced the more refined the water is. The logical course for the aquarist to follow would be to replenish the water with those elements which the water company has removed. However, it would be preferable to prepare aquarium water that contained a store of these elements that would last a longer time. At no time may even the smallest gap occur in the aquariums nutrient supply. Here we see clearly the structural difference between the artificial and the natural biotope. In tropical streams, nutrients are continually replenished. In the aquarium this only occurs through a water

1

change and the addition of fertilizer. Thus, we see that it is by no means easy to proceed on the basis of an observation of nature.

3.4.7.2.
Conclusions

It would be a fatal error to think that the imitation in the aquarium of »natural« water conditions would be a worthwhile pursuit. It is technically and practically entirely possible to produce »real Cryptocoryne water« synthetically, by taking distilled or de-salinated water and adding a salt mixture corresponding to that in the original stream. The aquarium industry could easily produce »original Cryptocoryne water imitation tablets« with the necessary composition.

Let us then consider this case. What would occur in this aquarium? The aquarist

Table: Water analysis from a Cryptocoryne Biotope				
Stream by Lam Pi Village				
Stream Region		1	2	3
Temperature °C		24	24.2	25
Conductivity μS 20°		19.4	20.2	22.2
Total hardness °dH (total earth alkali)		0.11	0.13	0.12
SK (Acid binding capacity)	mg/l	0.125	0.09	0.11
CO_2 (non aerated)	mg/l	3.0	11.0	10.0
CO_2 (aerated)	mg/l	1.5	2.0	2.0
CO_2 (actual)	mg/l	1.5	9.0	8.0
Organic Carbon	mg/l	2.3	2.6	2.0
Bicarbonate HCO_3^{1-}	mg/l	7.6	5.73	6.85
Chloride Cl^-	mg/l	–	2.9	3.3
Ammonium NH_{4+}	mg/l	0.02	0.06	0.04
Nitrate NO_{3-}	mg/l	–	0	0
Phosphate PO_4^{3-}	mg/l	0.088	0.028	0.019
Oxygen O_2		8.0	6.5	5.5
pH-value		6.9	5.6	5.8
rH-value		29.6	27.5	28.0
Iron				
Iron in solution	mg/l	–	0.22	0.32
Iron in precipitates	mg/l	–	0.05	0
Total iron	mg/l	0.14	0.27	0.32
Manganese Mn	mg/l	0.2	–	–
Calcium Ca^{2+}	mg/l	0.51	0.30	0.40
Magnesium Mg^{2+}	mg/l	0.18	0.13	0.21
Potassium K^+	mg/l	0.53	1.00	0.90
Sodium Na^+	mg/l	1.40	2.05	3.00
Sulphate SO_4^{2-}	mg/l	2.26	0.48	0.42

1: Waterfall lower part of source
2: *Cryptocoryne cordata* (photo page 59)
3: End region: *Crinum thaianum* and *Cryptocoryne ciliata* (see page 60)

who hoped to obtain good plant growth with the original cryptocoryne water would be very disappointed: The result would be nothing short of a catastrophe, for the plants would sicken and rot.

The explanation for this disaster is simple. In original water with such a limited amount of nutrients the plants would quickly absorb and exhaust the majority of them. After a short time nutrient gaps would occur and some nutrients would be missing entirely.

On the other hand, the stream of flowing water need only provide those nutrients which are necessary at any given time. The aquarium, no matter how strong the circulation still represents only a tiny amount of water. Yet in both cases plant growth must occur according to the same laws of nature.

In practice this means that we must be careful that the optimum amount of nutrients needed for plant growth is supplied from one water change to the next and that no gaps occur, for each nutrient gap can damage the plants or even occasion their loss.

The Liebig Minimum Law provides proof of this. According to this law, plant growth is determined by the one factor that is present at a minimum. Thus, optimal carbon fertilization is useless to aquarium plants if there is an acute lack of iron. In this case even worse can occur. For the combination of the stimulating effect of the CO_2 fertilization and good lighting, would lead to an even clearer and stronger iron chlorose.

If the lack of nutrients hinders plant growth and assimilation in the aquarium, plants will cease to produce the oxygen that is very necessary for the breathing and the health of the fish.

Unfortunately, tap water is not only considerably lacking in nutrients, but it does contain an over-supply of certain compounds. For example, the water company tolerates the presence of nitrate (which is the highest oxidation level of nitrogen), in drinking water, because it poses no health threat. In many areas an increased demand for sub soil water has lead to a considerably greater nitrate content, a condition that is most unfortunate for aquarium plant growth, since the fish in the aquarium already supply adequate nitrate.

An over-supply of nutrients can be just as damaging to plant growth as nutrient gaps. Surplus nutrients for example can prevent the plant's assimilation of those nutrients that are in short supply, or can lead to the formation of undesirable chemical compounds that, in turn, can cause severe plant damage. Examples of this are to be found in Chapter 3.6.9. Plant Diseases.

In addition, many tropical plants are not amenable to nitrate as a nitrogen source. The more so, since they have not »learned« to use this highest oxidized form of nitrogen because they are spoiled in their native environment by ammonium, which is much better for plants. There are indications that Cryptocoryne rotteness is caused by over fertilization with nitrate. Here too, see Chapter 3.6.9. – Plant Diseases.

To sum up, we have seen that contemporary tap water, while certainly accptable as drinking water, cannot be considered suitable for aquarium plants. Thus, we are faced with the problem of overcoming these ddifficulties in order to prepare healthy, usable, aquarium water in which both plants and fish will prosper.

3.4.7.3.
From Tap Water to Aquarium Water

All biotope studies have shown us exactly the composition of good aquarium water. Now we must put the knowledge gathered in the tropics into practice.

We begin with important and practical considerations since we must use tap water for our own aquariums. Special aquariums and nursery aquariums will be considered elsewhere.

Today's tap water not only contains large nutrient gaps, but its chemical compounds also do not resemble those in tropical streams. Corrections and additions are necessary. First, a good fertilizer developed specifically for aquarium use should be ac-

1

3

2

4

1 The »Liebig Minimum Law« also applies to the aquarium. Minimum law: Plants only grow healthy and optimally if all nutrients are available in the correct proportions. This was demonstrated by the research we did with aquatic plants.
1 Research (all 4 in a 4 compartment tank, color of pots differ, pots are seperated) Cabomba in hard water with additives (l. to r.)
a) only mains water
b) mains water + CO_2 fertilisation
c) mains water + CO_2 fertilisation + aquarium complete fertilisation
d) mains water + fertiliser, no CO_2
2 Same research after 3 weeks
a) all plants are chlorotic, most of them dying
b) plants grew longer but are chlorotic
c) full green and healthy plants
d) full grown but smaller because of lack of CO_2
3 Same research with Hygrophila polysperma
4 Same results with Cabomba aquatica.

quired. According to our knowledge, it must fulfill the following conditions:

- Nutrients that are in short supply or that are not present at all in tap water should be added, for example, potassium.
- Keep in mind that some essential nutrients are produced in the aquarium itself. For example, this may occur through the metabolican of fish and snails or through food remains. These nutrients are principally nitrate and phosphorous.

For this reason it would be entirely inappropriate to use fertilizer prepared for garden and balcony plants in aquariums. For these fertilizers consist chiefly of nutrients that are already in over-supply in aquariums and cause problems there. Over fertilization with these nutrients normally leads to severe plant damage. See Chapter 3.6.9. – Plant Diseases.

Aquarium fertilizer must contain the entire spectrum of trace elements that are important for plants as found in tropical stream analysis. The Liebig Minimum Law holds true for trace elements as well.

Aquarium fertilizer that satisfies all of these prerequisites, must be conceived on the basis of the water analysis of tropical plant water, and with extensive experimentation with aquarium plants under aquatic conditions. The test plants should be supplied with nutrients at different intervals and in different combinations over the course of a number of weeks and these plants should be tested, weighed, and measured. In this way the optimum cultivation method for aquarium plants can be determined.

The use of an aquarium fertilizer that has been developed along these lines is one of the most important steps toward a reproduction of optimal living conditions in an artificial biotope. This attempt to achieve quality however, can be furthered by other characteristics of a good aquarium fertilizer.

Earlier we mentioned that iron, manganese and several other trace elements are only water soluble for a short time. They oxidize in the presence of oxygen, precipitate and are then useless as plant nutrition. Immersed plants can only assimilate these dissolved nutrients through their leaves. In tropical streams the problem of these critical nutrients is solved by the permanently seeping nutrient sources. So the precipitated and exhausted nutrients are continually replenished by this ongoing fertilization.

A good fertilizer will take on this responsibility in the aquarium as well, by means of a chemical trick. There are chemical substances that bind and protect certain elements so well that oxygen can not touch them and precipitation can be largely avoided. These substances fare known as chelators or chelates.

Ethyldiamintetra acetic acid (EDTA) is one of many nutrient carriers which is commonly used for plant fertilization. Plants are able to take in nutrient complexes made with EDTA, to remove the bound nutrients such as iron et al., and to use them. A good aquarium fertilizer will contain this and other chelators in a well balanced and carefully tested combination of nutrients.

In order to achieve an equal, steady nutrient supply, aquarium fertilizer is only poured directly into the aquarium according to the dosage instructions, upon the initial establishment of the aquarium. Later fertilization occurs only during a change of water, and then the fertilizer is only added to the fresh water. Regular water change not only prevents the undesirable accumulation of nutrients, but also removes waste products of fish and plant metabolism.

3.4.7.4.
The Challenge of Nutrient Springs

The discovery of nutrient springs, and the observation that certain critical nutrients are continually replenished in plant water, led us to certain conclusions for the aquarium.

These critical nutrients are principally iron, manganese and other trace elements which are needed by plants only in very small quantities, but which when absent from aquairum water, lead to severe plant damage. The problem with these nutrients is that they have a toxic effect when present in large amounts, so over fertilization should be carefully avoided. However, they also precipitate quickly during oxidation. Because of their toxicity in large amounts,

they cannot be supplied with each water change.

The binding of these »critical nutrients« to chelators represented a tremendous breakthrough, and an enormous step in the care of aquarium plants. Many plants which are common today were unknown in aquariums a few years ago.

Recent studies have shown that there are conditions under which the supply of these critical nutrients can not be achieved from water change to water change, with the necessary continuity. The amount of oxygen, the pH value, plant mass, light, fish and salt content are all factors that influence the behavior of chelated nutrients.

Thus, the dosage to be added to the fresh water when changing water should be divided into daily portions.

Another better method would be to prepare a daily or a 24 hour fertilizer, like fish food, consisting only of the »critical« nutrients and to add it in doses. This should be combined with iron measurements because all trace elements behave like iron towards oxygen, pH value and other factors that determine their use and precipitation. An Fe content of 0.1 mg per liter is desirable, whereby it is important to remember that small traces of iron are present even in the absence of light. We believe that higher levels of iron such as 1.0 or even 2.0 mg per liter which is commonly suggested are too high and quite unnatural.

So called hose pumps with electrical dosage mechanisms have proven excellent for the dosing of daily fertilizers, because they guarantee an even and continuous supply of the critical nutrients.

3.4.7.5.
The Problem with Carbon

While the solution of the nutrient problem with modern aquarium fertilizer functioned ideally in the aquarium, one of the most important plant nutrients in the aquarium can not be pressed into tablets: carbon. Tablets can not be used because aquarium plants must be provided with carbon in a primarily gaseous form as free carbon dioxide, which is sometimes incorrectly identified as carbonic acid. Carbon is one of the most important plant nutrients, because along with light and water it is one of the 3 staple factors of plantlife. Thus before we take into consideration how carbon should be provided we must consider one of the laws of nature which permanently influences fish and plant life in the aquarium.

1 A typical leaching area in tropical water. Water with a high nutrient content is supplied.
2 In the aquarium, a Dosing pump can be used to achieve this continuous supply of nutrients.

3.4.8.
Oxygen by Photosynthesis

Many readers will still remember from their nature studies in school that chlorophyll, the green color substance in leaves, is responsible for producing an important synthetic material: glucose from water and carbon dioxide. Glucose then provides for the further building and energy metabolism of the plants. This process is called photosynthesis because it occurs under the influence of light.

But glucose formation is not the only result. Oxygen too is released by the plants into their environment. This is true for emerged as well as submerged plants i.e. photo synthesis also occurs in the case of submerged plants and oxygen is released into the water. Oxygen which the fish need to breath.

Because of the importance of photosynthesis we will look at it again in Chapter 3.9.

– The necessity of providing optimal light.

In second point of the pointers of success we indicated that it is very important for the aquarium that we reach or go beyond the point of oxygen saturation in the course of one day. Naturally other factors besides sufficient light play a roll here. Organic waste products, too few plants, too many fish, over feeding, poorly cleaned filters, etc. also consume oxygen.

Therefore it is important to carry out an O_2 control at regular intervals and in the case of a serious O_2 deficit to consider what may have been its cause.

---

1 Healthy plants that assimilate properly, give off oxygen in soluble form to the water. In some areas (mostly because of minute damage) this can be seen as small bubbles rising from the leaves.

1

3.4.9.
Carbon Content

There are many factors which must be taken into account with regard to the amount of carbon in water and specifically in aquarium water. While the amount of carbon in the atmosphere is almost unlimited, this is not the case in water. The cause for this is the multifaceted make-up of carbon. In water there is a particularly complicated carbon system from which the submerged plants can take the necessary carbon in various ways. For example:

- From the free gaseous dissolved carbon dioxide (CO_2)
- From carbonic acid molecules (H_2CO_3)
- Through the assimilation of bicarbonate in the form of ion pairs, for example $Ca(HCO_3)_2$
- Through the assimilation of HCO_3 in the ion exchange against another anion.
- When the pH value is higher through the assimilation of CO_3 (carbonate).

This list makes it clear that there is a much greater variety in quantity and quality of carbon provision in water than on land.

This list of carbon varieties is however, only of theoretical value with regard to the carbon needs of aquarium plants. For only the gaseous dissolved carbon dioxide (CO_2) is suited for use without complications by aquarium plants.

When the amount of free CO_2 in water diminishes a process called biogenic decalcification begins. Through this process the plants cover their need for CO_2 by taking their carbon from the bicarbonates (double carbonic acidic calcium). The pH value may rise to 9 or 10 during the course of this process. This could however have fatal consequences in an aquarium as we shall see later on.

In natural waters, streams, lakes and rivers a few types of plants exist in a large amount of water. However, in the aquaristic hobby we usually grow many types of plants in a relatively small container of water. These plants are however sometimes quite different in their ability to take the carbon they need from the available carbon systems. *Elodea canadensis* for example, is able to assimilate carbon from CO_3 and thus to raise the pH value to 10. While

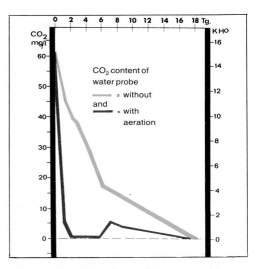

Figure: Free CO_2 always has the goal to try to equalize with the CO_2 in the air, meaning to escape from the water. Experiments have shown that this process is faster when the water is in movement, then when it is still. Our graphic shows how fast 60 mg/l CO_2 escaped from the water during our experiments.

the source moss *Fontinalis antipyretica* can only use free carbon dioxide. Other aquarium plants lie somewhere in between. Thus it becomes clear that there is considerable competition in the aquarium for carbon and that those plants which can sustain higher pH factors have an advantage over the others.

1 *Biogenic decalcification does occur in other areas than the aquarium too. Here the well-known example from the Pliwitzer Lakes in Jugoslavia. Water with a high carbonate hardness and CO_2 streams into the lake. CO_2 is removed by waterfalls. Lime and calcium compounds precipitate because of CO_2 imbalance and cover the stems leaves of the plants, roots and rock.*

Biogenic Decalcification

Some of our readers may be interested in the following proof.

We carried out a number of experiments

1

in order to test the ability of various plants with regard to the biogenic decalcification of a body of water. The results were as follows (see Table). Within 28 days a carbonate hardness of 14.7 sank to 3.4 with the addition of *Egeria densa*. Further values can be seen in the table.

Table

Values for the test water	SK 5.25	KH° 14.7[1]
1. Egeria densa	1.2	3.4
2. Myriophyllum heterophyllum	1.75	4.9
3. Carbomba aquatica	3.25	9.1
4. Sagittaria subulata	3.25	9.1
5. Cryptocoryne affinis	3.7	10.4
6. Cryptocoryne petchii	3.95	11.1
7. Ludwigia repens	4.35	12.2
8. Vallisneria asiatica	4.7	13.2

Light intensity 20 000 Lux

[1] Carbonate Hardness = SK (acid binding capacity) × factor 2.8

Our experiments showed that submerged plants first cover their carbon needs from free carbon dioxide because they need little energy in order to do this. When the free CO_2 is exhausted they take bonded carbon from the bicarbonates. Furthermore our studies showed that this process is dependent upon energy. *Ludwigia repens* and *Vallisneria asiatica* which showed very poor results during our experiment with light at 2200 Lux (see Table) were able to improve their performance considerably when the light was raised to 20 000 Lux. Under these conditions *Ludwigia repens* was able to reduce the acid binding capacity of the water from 5.2 to 1.8. Here the difference between »light« plants and »shadow« plants is clearly visible.

Our optimal aquarium system, however, offers all plants the same chances with regard to CO_2 availability.

3.4.11.
CO₂ Water Chemistry
3.4.11.1.
Carbon Dioxide has a double Function

In addition to its function as a plant nutrient, carbon dioxide is also a chemical equalizing component in the bicarbonate-carbonic acid system. The greater the amount of bicarbonate dissolved in water (or the higher the carbonate hardness) the more free carbon dioxide is necessary (see Table). If the amount of free CO_2 falls, calcium precipitates. This is a procedure

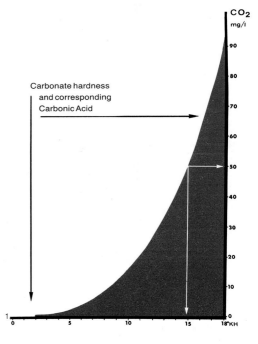

which can be observed in the aquarium through calcium deposits around the water surface, on the leaves, and in other places. This process is always accompanied with some rise in pH value. In addition carbon dioxide also has the tendency to escape from the water because it wants to become equal to the CO_2 concentration in the air. This effect can also be strengthened by any bubbling of the water, for example through the addition of airstones. This is one of the reasons that we recommend that the ideal water movement in the aquarium be achieved without using air driven water devices, under the water line. In this way the aquarium water will have a circular movement as opposed to a continuous whirling movement from below to above.

3.4.11.2.
pH and CO_2 Control

Because of the great importance for plant growth in the aquarium of optimal hydrogen carbonate – CO_2 balance, we believe that a continual control of this system is necessary. Although this control initially appears to be very complicated, it is really quite easy with the CO_2 test.

The indicator fluid of the test apparatus, which should be visible within the aquarium, takes on a different color according to the pH value. When it is green this shows us that the pH value lies in the neutral range 6.8 to 7.2 and that the CO_2 is being provided at an optimal level. When the fluid is blue the pH value is too high and the CO_2 supply is being interfered with. When the fluid is yellow the pH value is too low and the amount of CO_2 too high. According to our experience, when these CO_2 tests are run regularly without the benefit of CO_2 fertilization, a CO_2 deficit occurs. For us this means that the supply of CO_2 in the aquarium should be improved.

Quantitative CO_2 measurements will test the amount of CO_2 without difficulty.

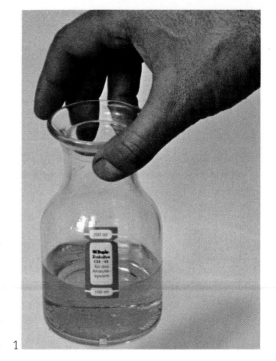

1

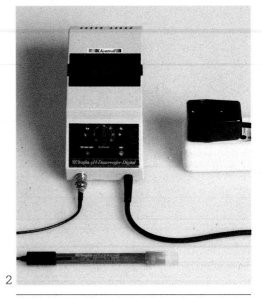

2

1 The CO_2 content of water can be found, not only through pH, but also quantitatively measured. Tests to do so can be found in tropical fish stores.

2 Modern pH continuous controllers can measure the pH accurately and control the supply of CO_2.
3 A hand held pH meter, measures the pH quickly in the aquarium, in streams and elsewhere.

3.4.11.3.
Criteria for Determining CO_2 Need

How CO_2 fertilization is to be carried out, is dependent on various criteria which have an effect on the need for free carbon dioxide in the aquarium. These criteria are:

Energy – Light

Light is the motor of plant assimilation. The stronger the light the more plant metabolism is stimulated. At the same time however, the use of nutrients is accelerated. Primarily the need for carbon increases, i.e. more carbon dioxide must be added to the aquarium water. This can be easily tested in the aquarium. If there is sufficient light the plants release oxygen as a sign of assimilation, and this can be observed through the little gas bubbles which form on their leaves. If at the same light intensity, the available CO_2 is raised or lowered the release of CO_2 to the leaves is correspondingly increased or decreased

Water Volume – The Size of the Aquarium

The performance of the CO_2 fertilizer device will vary according to the size of the aquarium and the resulting amount of water. Large aquariums have an advantage here as opposed to smaller ones: The chemical stability of the water is greater. Particularly the pH value, the amount of CO_2, and of carbonate content, can be kept more stable using the right CO_2 set-up.

Plant Mass – CO_2 Consumers

The third factor with regard to the consumption of CO_2 is the plant mass present in the aquarium, i.e. the actual carbon consumers. The more densely an aquarium is planted, the more CO_2 is needed. On the other hand dense planting guarantees a good or better provision of oxygen in the aquarium, and thus a better milieu for aquarium fish.

Furthermore the need for CO_2 is determined by the types of plants in the aquarium. Plants that grow fast such as *Elodea*, *Hygrophila* and *Cabomba*, to mention just a few, use considerably more CO_2 than plants which grow slowly such as *Anubias* and *Cryptocorynes*. The ratio of carbonates (carbonate hardness) an the amount of CO_2 plays a greater role in the

aquarium than in natural waters. This ratio is responsible for the pH value of the aquarium water (see Table 6.3). Since in contrast to natural waters there is a relatively large number of different types of plants in the aquarium, all of which have different optimal pH values and different CO_2 needs, but all of which can exist well in a neutral pH environment. We recommend that a neutral pH be achieved through CO_2 fertilization. Aquarium stores can provide sufficiently accurate measuring tests and measuring instruments in order to determine the carbonate hardness, the pH value and the amount of CO_2.

Other factors which affect the need for CO_2 are the amount of fish, the temperature, the substrate, the water movement, the amount of food, water change and care.

3

3.4.11.4.
Methods of CO₂ Fertilization

For many years CO_2 fertilization was much debated. It was only after the Second World War, when the aquarium hobby underwent a change, and the era of modern aquaristics began with the use of fluorescent light, HQL and HQI lights, and filter pumps which resulted in strong water movement in the aquarium, that it became increasingly evident that CO_2 was lacking in the aquarium and the search for suitable fertilizing methods began. This began with various »pioneer devices« which are no longer used today, and which were replaced by an elegant and economical CO_2 fertilizing method which is as follows:

1

CO₂ fertilization by means of a flow reactor

Through this method the aquarium water flows by means of a water pump over a cascade in a reactor tube, thus receiving carbon dioxide in a CO_2 rich environment. Almost all common aquarium sizes and mains waters with very high carbonate amounts can be optimally fertilized through choosing the correct reactor size, and by setting the device at the desired level of efficiency. This system also uses reusable bottles, in various sizes, pressure reducers with manometers and magnetic valves for on/off mode. The entire system can be assembled in a modular system, calminating to a fully automated CO_2 fertilization, with continuous pH control, whereby the desired pH value can be set at will, by means of a pH electrode.

1 Practical CO_2 bottles (CO_2 depot) in many sizes assure a continuous CO_2 supply.
2 In the reactor CO_3 and water are mixed efficiently.
3 Pressure device for automatic CO_2 supply.
4 A superbly contructed CO_2 test allows fast qualitative CO_2 availability control.

2

3

4

3.4.11.5.
Obsolete Procedures to yield CO_2

There are other procedures which yield CO_2 besides the one that we have discussed here, and we mention them in order to be thorough, and not because we believe that they are particularly useful.

One method employs fermentation in order to supply the aquarium with CO_2. Sugar from yeast dissolved in water yields carbonic acid. The disadvantages of this method are obvious. This CO_2 fertilization procedure requires much care and work. It is almost impossible to provide CO_2 in the correct dosages and then CO_2 occurs very rarely in its pure form.

This method of obtaining CO_2 however, is interesting for teaching purposes and does represent a possibility for beginners who want to undertake CO_2 fertilization in the aquarium in an economical manner. The method is acceptable as a temporary one, if sufficient care is taken. It is described in detail in Paffrath's »Bestimmung und Pflege von Aquarienpflanzen«, published by Landbuchverlag, Hannover.

We do not recommend CO_2 fertilization through the addition of mineral water which contains carbonic acid. This method does not guarantee a continual supply of CO_2, nor is it long lived. Furthermore, the concentration of salts which are present in greater or lesser quantities in mineral waters, have an uncontrolled negative effect on aquarium water.

Finally, we should mention the dubious factor of obtaining carbonic acid from marble. To do this a piece of marble is dissolved with hydrochloric acid, thus releasing CO_2. This method is entirely unsuitable for the hobby, not only because of its cost-prohibitive nature, but also because of the danger of using hydrochloric acid.

3.4.11.6.
Results of CO_2 Fertilization

CO_2 fertilization may appear very complicated to the reader, but an aquarium which is held at a neutral pH is worth the trouble.
- The aquarium plants will grow to be stronger, lager and more healthy because only through a sufficient supply of carbon are they in the position to make full use of the other available nutrients.
- The oxygen content of the water rises through CO_2 fertilization. Now the plants are able to assimilate optimally. This can easily be observed through the rising of oxygen pearls.
- There are no longer any unsightly calcium deposits on the leaves and the aquarium glass.
- The neutral pH value prevents dangerous ammonia-ammonium reactions, which occur at high pH values.

1

3.4.12.
Water Changes

Before we conclude this chapter we must come back to an important observation from the tropical stream: the current in flowing water. For many water plants this is vital for their life, because the current washes metabolic waste away and new nutrients are provided.

Good impeller and piston pumps can provide movement in the water, but the waste products of fish and plants are not removed from the aquarium. At best they are moved around the aquarium. They can not be removed from the aquarium by means of a filter and certainly new nutrients are not provided in this way.

There is only one remedy for this and that is a regular change of water. This provides two important things. First, surplus nu-

trients and nitrates which were not used or could not be used are removed, and secondly fresh nutrients needed by the plants are provided.

There is one rule here. Fertilize only upon installing the aquarium, and afterwards only upon a change of water.

At every water change fertilize only in accordance with the amount of water changed.

In this way undesirable and uncontrollable nutrient build-up in the water can be avoided, and a balanced nutrient level can be achieved. There is a further factor which clearly shows the great structural difference between the natural and the artificial biotope, right from when the aquarium is first set up and also when the water is changed.

As soon as it leaves it's source, water comes in direct contact with large amounts of organic deposits. Natural sedimentation, particularly in tropical streams, lakes and rivers is surprisingly high. Sediment formation up to 1.8 meters has been measured in these waters. These deposits consist primarily of organic material from plant remains and algae. It is decomposed by bacteria or small molds which ferment cellulose and then forms new organic materials. A permanent exchange of organic materials occurs between these sediments and water, these organic materials are of course not present in tap water.

They provide the fish with protective colloids for their skin and gills which make them less sensitive to germs, fungi, and various parasites.

In the aquarium many fish react to tap water, which does not contain these protective colloids, with visible malaise and lack of appetite.

We recommend therefore that this gap in tap water be corrected by the use of a suitable water preparation which should contain the protective colloids found in natural water, in addition to germicids in order to prevent the growth of skin and fin bacteria.

1 A good water conditioner protects the fish through slime protecting ingredients.

3.5.
Filtering and Movement

We have observed very many different types of water in the course of our studies in Sri Lanka (Ceylon), Borneo, Malaysia and Thailand. We have seen murky and clear water, standing water and heavily flowing water. Still, our chemical data were in agreement to a certain extent. Murky water during the rainy period contained almost the same concentration of nutrients

as the partially crystal clear water in the dry period.

Of course water plants suffer in murky water because of the strong filtering of light. But even this »poor growth« made us, as aquarists, quite pale with envy. Even the fish do not seem to mind the murky water very much, because it is during the rainy period that large amounts of organic substances and nutrients are swept into the pools which offer the fish optimal nutrition. Even the changes in water level from 1 to 6 meters were borne by the fish apparently without any difficulty.

In summary we can say that:
- The fish do not care whether the water is clear or murky,
- Quickly flowing water has a positive effect on nutrient exchange,
- Water composition remains quite constant despite relatively large irregularities,

1 Many aquarium plants grow in fast running waters. In the photo one can see Blyxa in a deep, fast flowing, clear stream, in Sri Lanka. But also Aponogeton, Vallisneria, Sagittaria, Crinum, Ceratophyllum, Limnophila and others, are plants from streams with good water movement. Cryptocorynes come from moving waters and disappear from streams and rivers when they approach lakes or tanks.

1

● particularly in the rainy period when the water level is high and, the tide regenerates the substrate of the stream by turning over the upper level of the substrate. We assume that in this way elements in this upper substrate level which have a negative effect on plant growth are washed away.

Technically of course, these observations can only be reproduced in the aquarium to a certain extent. It is correct that aquarium water should be clear water, and that in order to obtain this we are dependent on technology. But crystal clear water is not synonymous with good aquarium water. For example no matter how clear the water, the pH value as well as the amount of nitrate and phosphate can be too high, just as there can be too little CO_2 or iron. As a rule however, one can say that murkiness in an aquarium is always a bad sign. It is not only aesthetically displeasing, but it is usually an infusoria out-break brought about by too much food, algae blooming or chemical precipitation.

In order to prevent, and if necessary correct, these effects we must use filters. Naturally we cannot just filter out of the aquarium water, an oversupply of nitrate or phosphate, because the filter can only support the entire system, and cannot overcome these problems alone.

We may generally assume that filtering will result in the following:
● Mechanical removal of murkiness by means of a cotton, sponge or diatomeous earth filter,
● Softening of the water by means of artificial resin,
● Biological filtering through bacterial cultures in a wet, dry or trickle filter,
● Detoxification of the aquarium water through the use of carbon.

Because we discuss the individual aspects of filtering, we have to make it quite clear that water plants play a very important role in this respect, in our optimal aquarium. We can only understand this if we keep in mind what it is that the water plants do in the aquarium. For this reason the above list of filters can be expanded with the following important points:

1. Dry trickle filter, bacterial filtering
2. Filter cotton, fine mechanical filtering
3. Highly activated carbon, chemical filtering and detoxification of aquarium water. Water preparation
4. Ceramic filter; rough mechanical filtering.
5. Film filtering; fine and rough mechanical as well as bacterial filtering.

The water plants are responsible for:
● Release of oxygen when enough CO_2 is assimilated,
● Removal of nitrogen compounds,
● Reduction of bacteria found in free water (coli bacteria through tubifex feeding),
● Reduction of poisonous substances such as zyankali, arsenic, and prussic acid,
● Release of antibiotics and organic metabolic products for the health of the fish,
● Providing the substrate zone with oxygen,
● Rough mechanical filtering

In addition the plants are also placed in the aquarium for decoration and to protect the fish. So of course we must take the following measures in order to stimulate the plant growth and in no way to hinder it. We must also ask ourselves what more can be done with regard to the actual filtering of the aquarium water.

By now it must be clear to the reader why we indicate that filtering in our aquarium is only a support of the entire system.

1 *Cryptocoryne cordata (f. siamensis) in an aquarium setting. In nature they are found in fast running streams and areas.*

What does a healthy plant do?

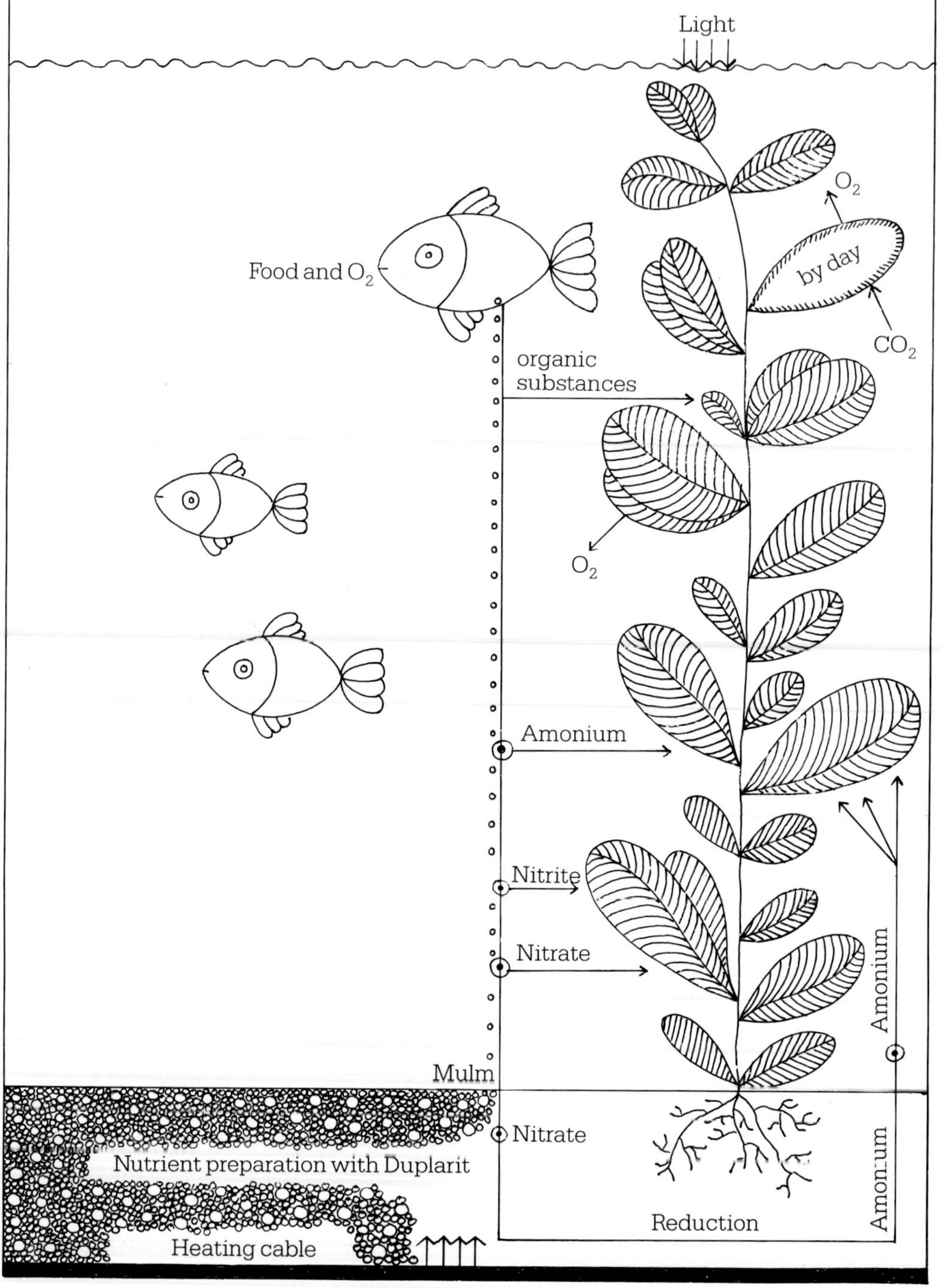

Light

O_2

by day

CO_2

Food and O_2

organic substances

O_2

Amonium

Nitrite

Nitrate

Amonium

Mulm

Nitrate

Nutrient preparation with Duplarit

Amonium

Amonium

Reduction

Heating cable

3.5.1.
The Meaning of Filtering

By filtering the water, we bring the water into contact with a material which, because of its structure, is able to retain suspended material, release other materials, and also to change the retained materials.

For example, rough or fine organic impurities such as excrements and plant remains decompose, after being trapped in the filter. This means that the water is clear, but it can be positively or negatively affected by the dissolution of the substances found in the filter. Thus it is clear that every mechanical filter can unwantedly become a biological filter. This occurs for example when a bacterial culture settles in a filter mass and the filter mass thus takes on biological activity along with the originally purely mechanical one. In the case of this process one must understand that large consumption of oxygen may occur. For this reason one should be careful that the water flow through of the system, no matter how it is constructed, does not go beyond the minimal level of 50 liters per hour in 100 liter of aquarium water.

All filter materials such as artificial resins, cotton, and carbon are effective filter masses for short periods, since they only have a limited capacity to absorb and to release. If the amount of time is not taken into consideration for which these filters will be effective, they lose or change their ability to function. Today we know that filtering in the optimal aquarium need only be a rough mechanical filtering, for it has the same function as a garbage collector as good aquarium water can, in the long run, only be obtained through good productive plant growth.

3.5.2.
Mechanical Filtering

At this point we should like to make it clear that the filtering of aquarium water to the extent that it is undertaken not by plants, but by technical devices, will only have good results if the following pre-requisites are fulfilled:

● The filter system should not remove any carbon dioxide from the aquarium water.
● The filter should be driven by an impeller pump or a submerged impeller pump.
● The rotatory capacity of the filter must be large enough to rotate the entire aquarium water at least once an hour.
● Changing the filter mass, which is necessary from time to time, should be a simple procedure, thus the rule that every filter is only as good as it is simple to care for.
● The whole system, including the over flow pipes and intake chambers, must be dependable for a long period of time.
● In our optimal aquarium the return flow of the filtered water back into the aquarium, should never pass through a diffuser or a sprinkler since this would drive out the carbon dioxide which is necessary for the plants.
● Above all else, the reader should be sure for his own interest, to take care of electrical security, which means isolating the motor casing well, and providing for sufficient protection against spraying water.

Some proven filter masses which also allow biological filtration are for example: filter cotton for fine filtration, foam for fine and rough filtration, bio-balls and filters for rough filtration. Because of the many different types of filter masses we would like to make the following suggestions to the reader, with regard to the use of a filter, so that in fact an optimal aquarium can be run.

When the aquarium is first filled with water, the filter can already be inserted. With the bio-balls care should be taken to insert a minimum volume of 5 % (e.g. 10 liters for 200 liters water content). Since, because of the initial instability of an otherwise well functioning aquarium, a slight murky appearance during the first 3 months cannot be prevented. The fine filtration masses mentioned above, such as filter cotton, active carbon and foam filters according to the filtration method used, can precede or follow the bio-filter, as needed.

During the course of the process the bio-ball filter takes on a fine filtration effect, since it must first be, in aquaristic jargon, run in. During this initial running in phase, it also begins bacteriological filtration, since bacterial cultures build on the synthetic framework and naturally also in the other in-line filter masses. These bacteria help the oxidation of organic substances, so that toxic nitrite cannot accumulate in the aquarium as it is immediately oxidized to non-toxic nitrate.

Good filter masses have the advantage that they supply perfect aquarium water, but they have the disadvantage that they must occasionally be changed. It would however be proposterous to assume for example, that a daily change of filter would have a major effect on aquarium hygiene. The material which accumulates in the filters dissolves so quickly that the concept of »frequent filter change« can actually be disregarded. When the visible flow of water diminishes, in most cases a change of the prefilter mass is sufficient.

This should be kept in mind particularly when new generation of impeller driven pumps are used. In this case the flow of water diminishes after a relatively short time, depending on the amount of dirt within 2 to 3 weeks, and the filter material used, must be changed without delay.

One thing that should be mentioned at this point is that, if because of electrical failure, the filter should be turned off over night and the water flow should stop completely, a aerobic bacteria will have died during this time. The bacterial function of the filter will have been destroyed.

This is not the case with the dry trickle filter which remains active up to two days in the case of electrical failure, and no water supply. However, this dry trickle filter needs a prefilter made of cotton or sponge. Because of its long lashing usefullness achieved in this manner, this filter does not result in much work for the aquarist.

In general, we recommend that a small part of the filter mass be left in the filter when the filter mass is changed in the hope

1 Peat moss that was very popular. When preparing water the drawbacks are to be found in the text.
2 Floss, made of Perlon, is hard to exclude from modern pre-and fine filters. It however clogs easily and has to be replaced frequently.

that the bacterial colony will quickly latch onto the new filter material. However, a new colonization with bacteria occurs automatically since a surplus of aerobic bacteria sticks to all water plants, to decorative objects and also to the surface of the substrate, and is carried by the flowing water and will thus quickly colonize the new filter material.

3.5.2.1.
Power Systems

Of course the water power systems which were used up to now, and which were driven by air are not suited for the optimal aquarium. A large amount of carbon dioxide is driven into the atmospheric air because of the great increase in surface through the formation of air bubbles. The loss of CO_2 in such aquariums would be so large that we would scarcely be able to replace it by using small CO_2 cannisters. Also these air-driven systems are unsuitable, because of their limited pressure. Only certain filter masses can be used with these filters, so that in general this type of system is useless.

In the last 6 years flow technology has developed strongly, in the form of impeller driven pumps and submerged impeller driven pumps. Today there are numerous water driven systems which can be submerged directly in the aquarium or used externally. These driving systems are quite secure and their practical operation is guaranteed in the case of all systems.

Generally we distinguish between three systems:

1. The submerged impeller driven pump.
The submerged impeller driven pump is a pump with the impeller submerged in the water, while the motor remains above the water zone. The advantages of the submerged impeller driven pump are:
a) high degree of efficiency and
b) the aquarium water is not heated by the warmth of the motor.

The disadvantage of this system lies in its operation. It is not always elegant to have a submerged impeller driven pump on the edge of the aquarium. The filter itself has to be placed below the impeller inside the aquarium. The submerged propeller driven pump is ideal for moving only the water in the aquarium. When the pump is installed, the filter should be left off and the impeller protected only by an strainer which would be attached to it.

2. Box filter
As the name implies the box filter, which is hung on the side of the aquarium, is driven either by a submerged impeller pump or by a built-in impeller pump. A back-flow pipe guarantees that the water that has been pumped in the filter system runs back into the aquarium. The advantages of this system are the following:

1 *Direct drive, high output pump, for use with larger aquariums and trickle, dry/wet filters. These pumps demonstrate particularly low noise level and generate no heat to the water (no heat transfer). Capacity is 3000 to 4500 litres per hour (1000 gallons or higher).*

1

a) Because of the simplicity of operation, without movement of hoses this system is particularly good for beginners.
b) This filter has a very high performance.
c) The filter mass can simply be changed by changing the cartridges.

But this filter system too has its disadvantages:

a) The placement of a filter on the exterior of the aquarium is not very aesthetic. In the case of closed and aquariums with outside decoration it is impractical.
b) A lesser disadvantage of the box filters is that they do not guarantee a directed stream of water because the flow of water back into the filter is in general very wide.

3. Impeller driven pump in a closed filter system:

There are two versions of the impeller driven pump:

a) the old traditional pump with an air cooled motor and power transfer through a magnetic disk. This motor is an A-synchronic phase motor with a very poor degree of effectiveness. The advantage of this pump however, is its relatively good sealing of about 1.5 meters at 0 head. This means that the performance curve stops at this height. Because the motor is air cooled, the aquarium water is not warmed.

Upon closer observation this impeller driven pump does have some small disadvantages. For example, its sensitivity to dust, the amount of noise it makes, and the fact that the pump is not protected from water fall because of the open motor operation.

This type of pump has been used in the hobby for the last 20 years with great success, and has proven its quality.

b) The other new type of impeller driven pump is completely encapsuled and protected and is completely water tight. The motor is called a synchronic permanent magnetic rotor. This pump does not have magnetic disk transfer and it's noise level is almost nil. In addition, this pump has only two bearings, as opposed to the 4 bearings of the previously described impeller pump.

---

1 Box filter with motor attachment. It is known for its long life and ease of operation.
2 Modern cannister filters in various sizes.

2

The motor is cooled by water and thus is constantly being lubricated. This construction is practically indestructible and the pump can be considered for very long term use. Its care and mounting are very simple.

Another characteristic of this new construction is that its capacity in terms of the amount of water turned over every hour, without filter opposition, is extremely high. In this regard, the amount of electricity used is quite low.

However, this new modern construction also has its disadvantages with which we must unfortunately live. Along with their great capacity to turn over water, all of these pumps have a very low head. For example, a pump of the older type is capable of about 100 liters per hour. When it's zero performance is about 240 liters per hour at a one meter head. A pump of the new type with an initial capacity of for example 500 liters at the same wattage, and with a head of 50 centimeters is also capable of only 100 liters per hour.

Since these new impeller pumps are partially or entirely encapsuled, and since part of their energy is turned into heat, the latter transfers to the aquarium water. In the summer time, if we are not able to keep the room temperature under 25° C, there will be a problem with overheating of the aquarium water.

A small cooling system would neutralize this disadvantage during the summer time in Europe, and in warmer countries.

3.5.2.2.
Canister Filters

Those canister filters, which are closed systems, outside of the aquarium, are all very much alike. They are characterized by a good position next to the aquarium, an intake hose from the aquarium to the filter, and a return hose from the filter to the aquarium. Many modern filters have built in hose clips and screws. Some manufacturers even offer built in automatic ball valves which permit these filters to be quickly removed from the aquarium, in order to be cleaned elsewhere.

In choosing a filter, a deciding factor is the amount of care the aquarist is willing to give. Normally the larger the filter size, the longer the filter will last, unless you choose a filter material which, because of its composition will not last very long, such as filter wool.

3.5.2.3.
Cooling Systems

In the presence of extreme temperatures, particularly in the summer, the aquarium water must be cooled. This will actively prevent damage to the plants and fish. Steady low temperatures, (25° Celsius) will maintain a balance and resultant balance of oxygen. Particularly in tropical countries, in which average temperatures lie between

1 Long lasting refrigeration/cooling unit with titanium parts. It is used specifically for cooling aquariums in warm countries. It can regulate the temperature automatically between 15° and 30° C.

27 to 30° Celsius, a cooling system is an important feature of an aquarium. Cooling systems have proven their worth where fish are kept for food, particularly in restaurants. Cooling systems are sometimes necessary for fish native to European waters as well.

In this connection, we should like to point out that bog wood placed in the aquarium may have the same effect as peat. In this case, we recommend a change of water, in order to remove the bog wood leachings from the water. Since, in general water is to be prepared with peat, a change of water is not practical.

3.5.3.
Chemical Filtration

Tap water, whether hard or soft, is only conditionally useful to keep and breed fish and care for plants. The use of a water preparation substance is not sufficient to neutralize the aggressiveness of the water. It is absolutely necessary that the water contains a minimum carbonate hardness of 3.5° dH. Previously, and until recently, fresh water was often filtered through peat in order to remove its aggressiveness. Today however, we know that the use of peat, besides this positive characteristic, also has its negative points.

3.5.3.2.
Activated Carbon

Dr. Kurt Kramer, a leading German aquarist, developed activated carbon using a gas mask during the Second World War, and adapted it for aquarium filtration. He had great success with this, and it was a useful discovery for the hobby. Today there are many different kinds of carbon. Basically, activated carbon can adsorb a certain amount of color matter and protein matter. Unfortunately there is no quality-norm standard, for activated carbon. For this reason, filter carbons are continually

3.5.3.1.
Peat

1. Peat softens the water in a relatively uncontrolled manner. If the water is soft i.e., if its carbonate hardness is around 3.5° dH, for example, peat cannot be used.
2. Peat colors the water, and thus reduces the light penetration by up to 50 %.
   For desired plant growth then, it is necessary to compensate for this disadvantage by providing double the usual amount of light.
3. Peat filtration provides unfavourable conditions for water plants in the aquarium. Humic and yeast acids in peat have a negative effect on growth, particularly in the first critical phase of the aquarium, e.g. during the first two months. Such obstacles should be prevented.

1 High capacity activated carbon of superior quality, for preparation of pure water. To be used for removal of medicine, algicides, albumin. When used one should afterwards re-adjust the fertiliser content of the water as it will be significantly lower.

being used which promise more than they can deliver. If carbon is used for the aquarium, it should be a high performance activated carbon and should comply with the following quality standards:

1. Have pH neutrality
2. Be in granular form
3. Have large surface, area for example 100 grams equal 9000 qm (sq. meters)
4. Be dust free
5. easy de-gassing
6. Have practical application, using a mesh bag

When should activated carbon be used in a fresh water aquarium?

a) When the water cannot be easily changed, or when fish medication must be removed from the water after the treatment of diseases.
b) When the water cannot be easily changed and it becomes necessary to remove yellow colouring (such as urea) from the water.
c) Activated carbon can also be used when, despite optimal care, sensitive plants demonstrate poor growth. For example, in the case of cryptocorynes. In practice it has often been possible to absorb the growth-preventing elements on activated carbon. But this is still in the research phase.
d) During breeding, when extremely clean water is necessary, the use of activated carbon is particularly interesting.

There are naturally disadvantages to the use of activated carbon in a freshwater aquarium with water plants. And these should be clearly seen. Activated carbon is capable of bonding with other ions, such as nutrients in the form of iron, copper, and phosphate. Since phosphate only benefits algae, it may be filtered out. We may also be generous and overlook copper. But in the case of iron and other trace elements there is a problem. However, with today's technology it is simple to measure the very smallest amounts with an iron test, and fertilization can easily be undertaken with liquid, daily, fertilizers.

High performance activated carbon has proven its worth for use in fresh and salt-water aquariums. It fulfills the above prerequisites and can be used immediately by submerging it into warm water at about 25° Celsius. In this way the air trapped in the activated carbon is forced out, and the carbon becomes immediately active. A mesh bag can be used to hold the carbon, and in this form it can easily be placed in an interior or exterior filter, or even for a short time in the aquarium itself in front of the outflow pipe of the filter pump. In a relatively short time the water loses its yellow tinge. When the tinge is gone, the activity of the carbon can be measured. The measurement can be done most easily by means of a sight probe placed diagonally through the aquarium. The carbon should be removed from the aquarium water when the water begins to take on a yellow tinge again, because in this case it means that the activity of the carbon is exhausted.

Previously carbon was reactivated by heating it in an oven at a very high temperature. This however, was an incorrect method and should not be practiced today.

3.5.3.3.
Artificial Resin Filtration

a) In the aquarium

Before artificial resin filtration is put into use in the aquarium, we should discuss what the goal of artificial resin filtration actually is.

1. Initially the goal was to reduce the carbonate hardness, and the total hardness. At first glance, a complete demineralisation of the aquarium seems quite appealing.

However this is not the case in practice. At the beginning the fish live in water of, for example, 10° dH. This hardness is reduced to, for example, 5° dH through the introduction in the aquarium of ion exchangers. Along with this however, many important nutrients are lost. Iron can be considered the indicator in order to provide the necessary fertilization. What happens though, when the water has to be changed. In this case the fish and plants experience an environment of 10° hardness, and then suffer when it drops to 5° total hardness. This of course is stressful. When any factor is not held stable (in this case the on-going stability of the water) the effect is negative.

2. There are also ion exchangers which take other substances, such as nitrate or phosphate, out of the water. These ion exchangers are simply contained in the filter. But as the name ion exchanger indicates, it exchanges something, for example nitrate for chloride. Thus, if the aquarium water loses nitrate, it gains chloride. We know however that in many situations the addition of chloride to the aquarium has a negative effect on the growth of water plants, and also that there are some kinds of fish such as Discus which do not like this.

At any rate, exact information should be required from the manufacturer of such ion exchangers so that the aquarist knows exactly what chemical reactions will occur in his aquarium. We reject artificial resin filtration in the optimal aquarium because it disturbs continuity.

b) Ion exchangers outside of the aquarium.

In many cases it is necessary to soften the water outside of the aquarium, for example with ion exchangers, in an exchange column. This however, can only be recommended at water hardnesses of over 25° dH total hardness. The fully de-ionised water can then be mixed with tap water, in such a way, that it fulfills the stated prerequisites for the degree of total and carbonate hardness. These exchange columns are generally used for breeding purposes. For the aquarist the use of such exchange columns can become very complicated, since the columns and the various exchange substances, such as for example, hydrochloric acid and caustic soda are often difficult and complicated to use.

We should mention here that the fear of hard water has disappeared with the introduction of carbon dioxide fertilization. At any rate modern CO_2 diffusion methods guarantee the desired neutral pH value.

3.5.4.
Biological Bacterial Filtration

Biological bacterial filtration means that aerobic bacteria help in the organic breakdown process in the aquarium. Normally, these bacteria are present everywhere in the aquarium, even outside of it in the filter systems. They cling to decorative material, sand, walls, filter baskets and even plants. However, it would be hopeless to depend on this type of bacterial filtration alone. Indeed the surface for colonization by aerobic bacteria in the aquarium, is simply too small. For this reason it is necessary to provide the aerobic bacteria with an area for colonization that offers a larger and more open surface. All filter sponges and floss on filter cotton are good candidates, and of course gravel or carbon. You will be able to identify the best filter material if you know the following prerequisites for biological bacterial filtration. Since aerobic bacteria are continuously consuming oxygen in the course of their useful work, it is necessary to guarantee the availability O_2 at all times. This can be achieved in 3 ways:

1. The structure of the filter material must be open and permeable.
2. The inner firmness of the filter material must be such, that it won't slide together and cannot clog.
3. The flow of water must be as great as possible, since this will provide the bacteria with a large amount of oxygen. (It is wrong to say, as is often the case, that the so-called bio-filters only work well, if the water flows slowly.)

Normally the so-called bacterial filter is used submerged. That is, in a completely water filled system. Today we use this technique less and less, as many begin to prefer a trickle filter. The trickle filter guarantees another very important point, because it is open from the top to the bottom, and from the bottom to the top. Surrounding air is blown from the bottom to the top against the flow of the water, which drips down. Thus oxygen availability is influenced not only by the water flowing from top to bottom, but also by the air from bottom to top.

In principal, the drip method is very old. Trickle filters have been used, with great success, for decades, in sewage technology. It is actually rather sad that the trickle filter was discovered so late for the aquarium hobby, and it is also regrettable that no one recognized this new trend in the book »Aquarium Hygiene« by Hellmuth Wachtel, which appeared in 1963, and which described an aquarium clearing apparatus on page 35. Today, we know that almost all filters which are part of a closed circulation filter (impeller pump filters, with a hose connection to the aquarium) are pure oxygen traps. These filters are also partially filled with incorrect filter material, which have a tendency to get clogged, so that they can only be regarded with great skepticism for use in aquariums.

It is particularly dangerous when these filters, for any reason, are turned off overnight, and then turned on again in the morning. The resultant fall in pH, and the complete loss of oxygen can have terrible results. In addition an oxygen-less, closed, exterior or interior filter, is a death trap for all aerobic bacteria. Aerobic bacteria die in this type of filter because the water flow is stopped. (Lack of oxygen). The trickle or drip filter is different. With this type of filter system, if there should be a power stoppage, and the water flow cannot be maintained, the results are not tragic, since there is no clogged material in a drip filter, and thus the oxygen supply by the air, between the individual filter particles, can take place. The activity of a trickle filter, or drip filter, can be so great, that even dead fish which were not discovered in a normally stocked aquarium, can actually be consumed by the bacteria. Aerobic bacteria do not only need oxygen in order to live, as energy in order to develop. They do of course need nutrition in order to sustain themselves and multiply. Over the course of time, a so called balance occurs in the aquarium. i.e. as many bacteria develop as are necessary to take care of the existent organic load. If this load should become greater over a short period of time (e.g. Aunt Emma takes care of the feeding during the vacation), problems may occur because the bacteria cannot deal with the oversupply of organics. There is an elegant trick which can prevent this dilemma, whereby shortly before a vacation, the rate of feeding is slightly increased. The bacteria get used to his »excess« and multiply. At the beginning of the vacation period Aunt Emma can then go ahead, and use the entire can of food.

We should mention one more point. A drip or trickle filter is able to provide a minimum oxygen saturation of 80 to 100 percent on a continuous basis, day and night. In closed filters, however, the oxygen content may fall to thirty or even twenty percent. Thus the trickle filter is a rediscovered practice in aquaristics. However, at this point we wish to mention other opinions and experiences, even if some are not always in favour of the trickle filter. First there is the opinion that the trickle filter is a so-called »carbon dioxide« trap, since the counter-flowing air forces carbon dioxide out of the water.

We have also had this experience ourselves. The trickle filter, while it does not ac-

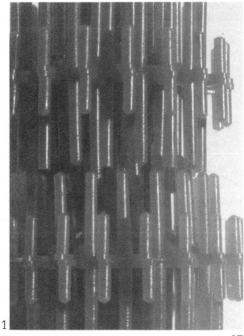

1 The Dupla Bioball is a superior quality material to fill drip/trickle or so-called dry/wet filters, and provides large area for the optimum growth of aerobic bacteria in the trickle filter (1 gallon = 21.5 square feet of surface area).

tually consume CO_2, is capable of removing carbon dioxide from the system. Of course bacteria provide CO_2 in the course of their breakdown process, but not enough to make up for the loss of CO_2. A loss of CO_2 is particularly evident in the case of soft water. Since soft water however does not need much carbon dioxide, this is not tragic. The loss of carbon dioxide in the trickle filter will however not be noticeable when using the new, modern, CO_2 diffusion processes.

It has also been said, and can partially be proven, that the filter is a so called nutrient trap. At first glance this is also understandable, since the oxidation of nutrients in a system like this, through oxygen and bacteria, occurs under ideal conditions. If we take iron as an indicator, we see clearly that the iron concentration is reduced unusually quickly during the initial use of the trickle filter (and sometimes also in a newly established aquarium.) The decrease can be explained as follows:

a) Newly set-up aquariums use large amounts of iron, but after 4 to 6 weeks a so called buffer system takes over, and the depletion of iron is reduced considerably.

b) The so-called nutrient trap during the initial stages of the trickle filter, can thus be explained. Since bacteria need iron during the running-in period i.e. while the filter is being heavily colonized, the need for iron is greater than later. After a period of at most 6 weeks, this phenomenon will disappear. Thus during this initial phase the aquarist must be patient, and give the bacteria and the aquarium what they need. Increased iron fertilization and measurement are absolutely necessary, in order to provide an interior balance in the aquarium.

3.5.5.
The Trickle Filter

Although the trickle filter technique is an old technique, it was only recently rediscovered. We would like to explain how the trickle filter functions with an example.

Number (1) in the sketch to the right is the filter intake through which by means of an overflow the water can flow from the aquarium either directly, or through an overflow pipe in the case of an aquarium with a hole. The dirt first collects in the upper pre-filter. The water then runs into the second chamber, and falls onto a fine sieve (3), which has the property of spreading the water as evenly as possible over the entire bio-ball surface. From here it falls through a sieve into the actual trickle body (4) which is filled with bio-balls. The water then drips down through many detours over the bio-balls. The trickle filter filling lies on a rough sieve that prevents the bio-balls from being submerged in the lower water level. One can do without the sieve, if one does not want to take the trouble to build in such a plate.

There is a diffuser (5) in the lower part of the filter, which sends air by means of a membrane pump, counterflow to the water, continuously from below to above, through the entire trickle filter column. In order to avoid evaporation, the trickle filter must be air-tight at the top (1). You can put the necessary air-vent at the top and this air directing system can be introduced into the lower area. It is here, in the lower area where air is diffused and the resulting condensation is then trapped by the water. The dividing disk (6) has the task of forcing the escaping air to rise through the trickle filter.

Sedimentations are filtered out through a fine filter box (7). A corresponding pre-filter made of sponge makes sure that absolutely no dirt finds its way into the pump (8, 9).

Using this technique, it is important to have a float switch in the water which will turn off the pump if the water level drops, in order to prevent at all cost a dry running pump.

When first running the filter the lower chamber has to be completely filled with water. Next the pump can be powered and the water pumped up into the aquarium. The water level in the aquarium rises automatically and the overflow brings the overflowing water back into the filter. At any rate, care should be taken that in the case of a power stoppage the reservoir of the trickle filter can hold the water that the overflow of the aquarium sends down.

Any professional pet store will be able to custom design, or build, a trickle filter for your aquarium according to this rough scheme.

We should like to mention one very important advantage. This trickle filter filled with bio-balls and with the in-line fine filter chamber, is able to reduce nitrate in a fresh water aquarium. The bacterial reduction occurs in the in-line fine filter chamber (7) in which many anaerobic (oxygen free) zones occur because of the very densely packed cotton. We have reduced this fine filter chamber, so that 80 % of the water flow occurs without filtering effect, and 10 to 20 % goes through this fine material. Since the chamber is very condensed because of the presence of dirt, oxygen free zones occur after the filter has been running for 4 to 5 weeks. The facultative anaerobic bacteria which have colonized this area need an oxygen part of NO_3 (nitrate) as energy source. Part of the nitrate is therefore reduced, and released into the air as N_2 (nitrogen in the form of a gas). The reduction of nitrate seems to be almost complete.

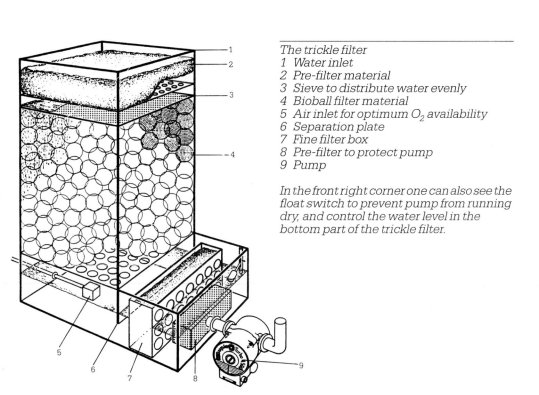

The trickle filter
1 Water inlet
2 Pre-filter material
3 Sieve to distribute water evenly
4 Bioball filter material
5 Air inlet for optimum O_2 availability
6 Separation plate
7 Fine filter box
8 Pre-filter to protect pump
9 Pump

In the front right corner one can also see the float switch to prevent pump from running dry, and control the water level in the bottom part of the trickle filter.

1

1 *With the introduction of the Bioball, a new generation of trickle filters has arrived. Many practical applications have seen the market, and can be stored underneath the aquarium in the cabinet. In the photo one can easily see the filterchamber and the float-switch protecting the pump. Pet stores can have these units built for their customers.*
2 *Water return from a filter unit.*

3.5.6.
Water Movement

Anyone who desires an optimal aquarium already knows how important good water movement is. A good impeller or piston pump is part of modern filter technology. However, despite the good performance of today's motor filters, we seldom achieve the desired turnover of between 200 to 1000 liters per hour in a 200 liter aquarium. Thus it is necessary to install an additional submerged impeller pump in addition to the actual filter, which will be placed either externally or internally. In this case, the water is only sucked in and pushed back in the

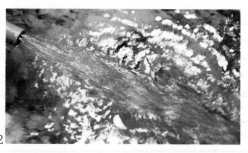

2

aquarium under heavy pressure, without any filtration effect.

This technique has the following advantages:

● Fish feel much better when there is a strong turnover in the aquarium, and they live in schools, as they do in nature. Because of the continuous exercise and swimming against the flow, they grow stronger and use their food better.
● There are no warm or cold zones in the aquarium because of the strong turnover.
● Through the quick changing of the water on the plant leaves, new nutrients are continuously being provided and nutrient oversupplies washed away. All plants react very positively to this.
● The current which is produced by these extra pumps, brings about leaf movement and as a result the leaves grow considerably stronger.

Incidentally, these positive results nearly correspond of course to the natural habitats of plants and fish, even in our artificial aquarium biotope. Optimum conditions can only be achieved through the greatest possible duplication of the natural environment.

3.5.7.
Surface Skimmer

The surface skimmer is a very helpful instrument which has come on the market in the last few years. It sucks in only the surface water regardless of the water level. There are two important advantages to this:

1. Dirt swimming on the water surface, such as micro algae, infusoria, grease (mould layer) is sucked in and led to the filter.
2. The care of a surface skimmer is much simpler than that of a deeply submerged filter basket. We wish however to point out the small disadvantage of carbon dioxide loss when the water in the vacuum pipe falls.

3.6.
Aquarium Plants

An attractive aquarium which serves as room decoration will contain healthy and decoratively arranged plants. In this chapter we will consider more closely plants for aquarium use, but we do not intend to provide a complete selection of all aquarium plants, but instead want to show the way to the Optimal Aquarium.

Furthermore there is already sufficient literature which describes in detail the entire spectrum of aquarium plants.

1

Basically, we see the plants as a building block in the biological unit »aquarium«. As such, the plants serve important and unique functions. We believe that when aquarium plants are considered only as decoration, this is incorrect and often harmful to the health of the fish.

The use of plastic plants is a terrible mistake and has nothing in common with serious fish-keeping. Fish which must live in an aquarium filled with artificial plants, lose all of the advantages which we describe in Chapters 3.6.3. to 3.6.6. We are of the opinion that aquarists, who in addition to plastic plants also fill the aquarium with

1 Red aquarium plants, e. g. Alternanthera types make fine contrasts.

other artificial paraphernalia, such as divers, sunken ships, etc., should also use artificial fish. Perhaps with a motor so that they'll move.

Only a successful combination of fish and plants in the aquarium creates an atmosphere in which both feel well. Fish and plants are not opponents or competitors in the aquarium, but rather partners whose existence needs to complement one another ideally.

3.6.1.
Plant Growth in the Aquarium

Surely we all agree on one point. An aquarium is only beautiful if the plants grow well and are decoratively arranged. In other words, when they make a cared for and healthy impression. No matter how beautiful the fish, an aquarium without plants does not allow them to show themselves to their best advantage. More important however, the fact is that this type of aquarium does not provide a healthy environment for most fish.

For this reason we should like to give the reader a number of suggestions which, with the help of proven techniques, care, and cultivation methods are almost guaranteed to create an optimal environment for plants and fish in his aquarium.

However, we should like to begin this chapter with a warning. The reader who has been at home in the aquaristic scene for a somewhat longer period of time, is used to hearing »But that's all nonsense. Come look at my aquarium, you'll see plants there and I don't do anything except occasionally replace the evaporated water«.

In fact, such aquariums, for which »nothing« is done, do exist and sometimes have »fantastic« plant growth. If the reader has time and desire, he could try to imitate such an aquarium. At that point he will realize that these aquariums cannot be duplicated.

Yet the ability to replicate is the most important pre-requisite for an Optimal Aquarium. Beautiful aquariums with heal-

1 *Cryptocoryne becketii*
2 *Rotala mallichii left, Cabomba caroliniana right*
3 *View of a large aquarium.*

3

thy plant growth have always existed, but an »aquarium with guaranteed success« has never existed. Far too often success depended on chance. At best the owner had a little bit of an idea.

If however, this aquarium broke down one day, or for any other reason had to be newly erected, the results were always the same. If the Aquarist attempted to achieve the same success in the same manner as before, very rarely was he able to cultivate the same splended array of plants. His belief as to why his plants had grown so well previously was not confirmed in repetition.

However you should not let yourself be discouraged as yo begin your way to the Optimum Aquarium.

3.6.2.
Plants with a Strong Will to Live

One of our ideas for the Optimum Aquarium is that healthy plant growth in the aquarium is always be »duplicated« and independent of the tap water used. We have a very important ally in our attempt. The plants themselves. Like all living things, they have a great desire to grow and to flourish. They possess a strong instict for self preservation, but when we see, in spite of this, so many aquariums with poor plants or perhaps without any aquarium plants whatsoever, we must conclude that the environment in these aquariums is hostile for the plants.

Actually this is easily understood. No matter how large the aquarium is, in comparison to the natural environment, whether it be a stream, lake or river, it contains only a tiny amount of water. For this reason alone the conditions of life in our aquarium can go from one extreme to the other in a very short period of timo.

As we mentioned above, the aquarium is an artificial environment and structurally much too small to allow the automatic development of the famous »biological balance« which would provide the plants living in the aquarium optimum conditions of life. For this reason it is necessary to produce an environment healthy for the plants

1

2

with the help of technical and chemical methods. The pre-requisite for this, however, is exact knowledge of the natural conditions, and the rules which can be derived from them. For years we occupied ourselves with learning these rules.

After numerous experiments with various nutrient combinations, and with hormones we wanted to study the water plant environment in which the plants had learned to exist, over the course of a long history of development, i.e. in their natural native environment. We undertook intensive investigation of the water and of the substrate. During the different seasons, i.e. during the rainy period when the streams had high water, during the dry period and during the normal period and we also carefully registered light and other environmental factors.

3

We came to the conclusion that the data which we had gathered here could not be transferred directly to the aquarium. After all, the conclusions which we came to on the basis of our investigations would have to take into account the different structure of the aquarium as opposed to the natural waters.

Let us consider here the biological functions of aquarium plants.

4

5

The plants in illustration 1 to 5 are particularly well adapted to provide the aquarium with oxygen right from the beginning, and thus provide optimum aquarium conditions.

3.6.3.
Plants as Providers of Oxygen

First of all, plants provide the oxygen which the fish need to breathe. The oxygen which is released by the plants comes from the photosynthetic process which we described briefly in Chapter 3.4.8. An O_2 measurement can easily test the amount of oxygen in the aquarium. Regular oxygen measurement is an excellent method to determine if the aquarium is functioning perfectly, biologically.

In a well-established aquarium, the oxygen saturation should be 50 to 60 % in the morning, but at about mid-day should be about 100 %. While this can be measured, it can also easily be seen through the fine oxygen pearls on the plant leaves which rise in the aquarium. These O_2 bubbles only occur when the aquarium is saturated with oxygen.

If however, the point of oxygen saturation in an aquarium is not reached for an entire day, this is usually caused by the following: either there is too little light; or the CO_2 content is too low; or another plant nutrient is lacking, or the water is too organi-

cally loaded. In such a case a change of water would be necessary.

Here we must mention one objection. It is incorrect, although it is often stated in even recent aquaristic literature, that oxygen can be introduced into the aquarium through chemical means, just as well as through plants. It is a fact that no air stone or oxidator, no matter how expensive, can provide oxygen to the aquarium as optimally as can healthy assimilated plants. Plants are even in a position to cause oxygen sufer-saturation. This is particularly the case in free waters with extreme sunlight, and in aquariums with very strong light.

Water plants are superior to technical ventilation etc., because they provide the water with oxygen in a dissolved form and only release it in fine pearls, once saturation is attained.

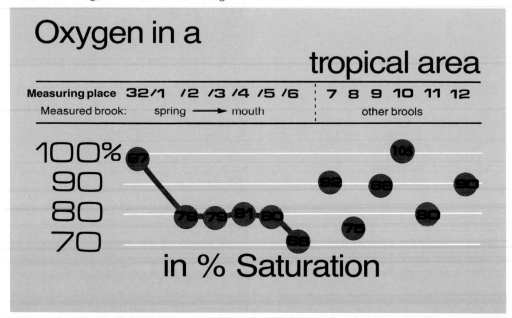

3.6.4.
Plants for Health and Hygiene

Healthy aquarium plants keep the aquarium water largely free of germs and are hygienic. There are now scientifically proven reasons for the observation that fish illnesses occur much less often in planted aquariums which are growing well, than in aquariums which are provided »mechanically« with air. Here aquaristics can profit directly from the attempts undertaken by Research Institutes to undo the damage done to the biosphere as a result of dense population and industrialization. The relevant experiments assume that many plants take not only water, mineral salts and carbonic acids from their environment, as classical botany teaches, but also take in and process large amounts of organic carbon compounds. Among these carbon compounds, are poisonous and dangerous elements.

A few years ago the Max-Planck Institute, in Krefeld, attracted a great deal of interest, with its attempts to reduce Bacterium coli and other germs, through the use of higher water plants. These germs were killed off so quickly that the observed phenomenon led to an expansion of this re-

1–3 Plants do not only provide oxygen for bacteria and fish, but they remove poison and noxious compounds from the water. Scientific research has demonstrated that plants remove disease germs from the water.

2

1

3

search. Experiments with water plants in sewers are being carried out today, not only in West Germany but also in Holland, Romania, and Israel. As a result of these attempts we have learned that water plants remove not only phenols from heavily loaded water but cyankali, carbolic acids, detergents and that a number of bacteria can be fought off with water plants. We have learned too from Göttingen's Institute for Soil Science that duckweed and other water plants are able to release a highly effective anti-biotic.

As responsible aquarists who wish to have a piece of living nature in our homes, we simply cannot afford to ignore these points from science and research.

The Optimum Aquarium that we are recommending in this book is thus quite consciously based on dense plantation.

3.6.5.
Plants against an Over-Supply of Nutrients

As we have mentioned numerous times before, an aquarium displays some structural weaknesses in nutrient provision, which we must correct. One of these weaknesses is the often too high nitrate content in the

1 The open aquarium also allows top views of the plants: Javafern, Microsorium pteropus
2 Hygrophila salicifolia
3 Rotala macrandra needs tall aquariums to grow well. In shallow aquariums it floats quickly on the top surface.

108

water. In Chapter 3.6.9. under Plant Diseases we will go into this again.

One measure against too high a nitrate content in water, is very dense plantation with quickly growing plants such as *Rotala indica*, *Rotundifolia*, types of *Vallisneria* and *Sagittaria* as well as *Hygrophila difformis*, *Egeria densa* and many others. *Riccia fluitans* is also very helpful in reducing any over supply of nitrate.

At this point we should also consider the benefits of duck-weed often disregarded by aquarists.

With their rapid rate of growth and reproduction, they have the highest substance production for a given period of time. There is no land plant which achieves this speed. Because of their high rate of reproduction, they also consume a large amount of those minerals and nutrients which can easily reach toxic levels in water, mainly nitrate, phosphate, etc. For this reason duck-weed water have become interesting for science, and are being used increasingly in water cleansing, processing, drainage channels and the like.

This interest on the part of Water works has caught our aquaristic attention. For years there have been a few portions of duck-weed in our aquariums. They represent a certain quality control for the nutrient contition of the water. If the duckweed grows large and green, the »nutrient clima« for the other aquarium plants is positive. If however, they remain small, or are yellow or brown, this should be cause for great alarm.

By using a net during water changes one can quickly make sure that the water surface is not be too densely colonized.

In this regard we should like to point out the practice of many aquarists of letting the roots of potted plants hang into the aquarium water. A favorite plant for this is the *Monstera deliciosa* or other types of

1 *Hygrophila difformis* is one of the most beautiful and efficient aquarium plants.
2 *Cabomba caroliniana*, originally from South America, has in the meantime become quite cosmopolitan. Here seen in black waters in Malaysia.
3 *Sagittaria graminea var. graminea*, the grass-like plant.

philadendrun, which can remove nutrients from the aquarium water through their free roots.

3.6.6.
Plants as »Cleaners«

By releasing oxygen through their roots many plants keep the substrate of the aquarium free of decaying areas. At the same time, they prevent the build-up of marsh gas in the substrate, and also prevent it's becoming black. Plant growth in black substrate is not possible. Healthy plants can however guarantee that the substrate of an aquarium never becomes black. A well cultivated plant group in an aquarium can actually be considered as an aquaristic »cleaning team«.

3.6.7.
Initial Planting – do it right

Many of the marsh and land plants which are for sale, cannot fulfill the functions necessary in aquaristics. Many of them are not without attraction, for they are sometimes quite colorful and bizarre, but they simply will not grow under water. They rot after only a short time. However, the colorful display in stores has already tempted many Aquarists to buy these plants. Thus some spotted *Dieffenbachia* ended up growing in the window sill where it certainly belonged, more than in an aquarium, and became a splendid example of its type. If you consider that this plant would have suffered a rather uncertain fate in the aquarium, you have to wonder why such plants are offered for aquarium use anyway.

However, the choice of plants suitable for the aquarium, fulfill their biological functions only under certain conditions. These conditions, furthermore, are often not at all or only partially present in practice.

A newly set-up aquarium is in a critical phase. The plants are not yet able to function because the roots have either been cut, or only a stem was planted to begin with. The plants metabolism and assimilation are still so weak, that they cannot release oxygen into the water.

1 An aquarium aesthetically arranged based on a planting plan worked out in advance.

1

In this beginning phase, in which the plants must first grow new roots, the aquarium is in a danger phase. Blue algae can easily build and that endangers the entire aquarium. As we will see in Chapter 3.7. algae is always an indication that the aquaristic balance is disturbed, or has not yet been reached.

It is tempting to compare the beginning phase of an aquarium with starting a car. When a car is started the automatic part or in some models still, the choke, releases a very rich fuel mixture which enables the car to start easily. This type of help is also needed in newly set-up aquariums.

The best way in which to overcome the critical beginning phase of a new aquarium, is to plant the aquarium densely with fast growing and well rooted plants. Fortunately these plants are abundantly and affordably obtainable on the market.

If we combine this with optimal light and nutrient conditions, we can guarantee good »soil processing« by the plants from the very beginning. If we are not successful, and the soil becomes black or decays, we have passed up the chance for healthy plant growth in the aquarium.

If however, the critical initial stage has been survived, more problematic plants, which need longer growth time, can replaced in the aquarium with the plants which have grown well. Thus it would be a mistake to plant a new aquarium with cryptocorynes or other problem plants, in large numbers.

The family of cryptocorynes should be »black-listed« for the first three months of a new aquarium, and only very few should be used. They can be planted in larger numbers when a second planting takes place.

This suggestion depends of course on the willingness of the Aquarist to think differently than he is accustomed to. For in many cases aquaristic engagement goes all the way and the Aquarist is prepared to invest a great deal of money in technical accessories, but becomes a miser when it comes to buying plants. Three *Ludwigia*, two *Vallisneria*, two *Myriophylla*, and one or two *Cryptocorynes* or *Aponogeton* are a poor beginning for a beautiful aquarium.

Usually, this is how most Aquarists who have been quickly disappointed with their aquarium and either sell it, or in frustration put it in the cellar, have begun.

When calculating the cost of an

1

aquarium, the amounts to be spent on plants should be reckoned somewhat more generously. The reader who has paid attention up to this point, knows already that the filter for example, need not be as large as originally planned. There are for example, successful Dutch plant aquariums which have no filter at all, proving that healthy plant growth can be an economizing factor. So one shouldn't economize when buying plants.

To the left we have drawn up plant lists for two aquariums of different size, as examples for aquarium planting according to our method. The plantating schematic will be considered again in Chapter 3.11. »Decoration«.

The optical impression made by a densely planted aquarium is very effective and pleasant for the observer. It is also possible that a companion, who has previously

---

1 *Micranthenum umbrosum, well placed in front of Bacopa amplexicaulis. This photo also shows that plants are better in groups, and that single ones would be lost.*

Planting schematic

Example A
Aquarium 130 × 60 × 45 (351 liter)

50	Echinodorus tenellus
30	Vallisneria americana
20	Didiplis diandra
20	Hygrophila polysperma
10	Heteranthera zosterifolia
10	Limnophila sessiliflora
10	Hygrophila corymbosa
10	Rotala indica
10	Rotala macrandra
5	Echinodorus parviflorus od. portoalegrensis
5	Lobelia cardinalis
5	Microsorium pteropus
5	Hygrophila angustifolia
2	Aponogeton crispus
2	Nymphaea lotus

Example B
Aquarium 160 × 65 × 50 (520 liter)

150	Echinodorus tenellus
70	Vallisneria americana
60	Hygrophila polysperma
40	Didiplis diandra
40	Limnophila sessiliflora
40	Rotala indica
30	Rotala macrandra
30	Heteranthera zosterifolia
30	Hygrophila corymbosa
20	Echinodorus parviflorus od. portoalegrensis
20	Lobelia cardinalis
20	Microsorium pteropus
20	Hygrophila angustifolia
4	Aponogeton crispus
4	Nymphaea lotus

observed the planning and activity with some distrust, will become more positively disposed in the face of success.

There are other factors which must be taken into consideration when making up a plant list for the first planting. The Aquarist must distinguish between plants which remain small, and therefore are suitable for the foreground, and those which will grow bushy-like for the side and back walls of the aquarium, and which can also be placed at important points in the aquarium, to provide a visual point or be eye catchers, and plants which, because of their size and the space they take up, can only be used as so called solitary plants.

1 Dense planting is possible using correct and adequate lighting techniques.

3.6.8.
Planting Plan

In this stage in the development of the aquarium we must fight against the temptation to be careless in planting the aquarium. We must admit here that we too have occasionally planted impatiently and without a set plan. However, this always has a negative affect on the impression made by the aquarium as a whole.

Furthermore, it is important to co-ordinate the biological demands made on the aquarium plants with the aesthetic effect they are to have. These considerations should not begin in the aquarium itself, but on paper, which means that we must make up a planting schedule. The reader should not consider this a superfluous and pedantic triviality. The most experienced Aquarists always work on the basis of a planting schedule which they have sketched out.

2

2 Cryptocorynes should possibly not be used in the first aquarium planting. Once the aquarium is run in properly, they can be included.

Our schedule, however, will take one additional aspect into account. The phases of initial and second planting. Thus we plan from the very beginning to replace fast growing plants (filler plants) with more demanding plants at a later date.

In short it is important when setting up a beautiful aquarium, that the plants be placed according to a certain order, which takes into account such aesthetic considerations as color, form, and height contrasts. Large leafed plants such as *Cryptocoryne cordata* or *Aponogeton ulvaceus* should be placed next to smaller leafed plants such as *Rotala rotundifolia* or *Limnophila sessiliflora*. The dark brown leaves of *Barclaya longifolia* contrast nicely with the light green leaves *Cryptocoryne lucens* or the light green Brazilian water navel *Hydrocotyle leucocephala*. Plants with smooth leaves such as *Vallisneria* or *Sagittaria* belong next to such curly wavy plants as *Aponogeton crispus*. Other examples for contrasting leaves are the conifer like American Water Hedge *Didiplis Diandra* with a completely bordered Cryptocoryne or the feathery Cabomba types with Alternanthera, Hygrophilia or Ludwigia.

These few examples of color contrast, and of leaf differences, show that there are an endless number of variations which can be added to with resinous pine wood and stones in order to develop a beautiful aquarium. Certainly several weeks will go by and improvements and corrections will be undertaken before the aquarium looks as it finally should. If the reader creates the correct biological and technical con-

ditions, as described in this book, he is guaranteed long term success with this system.

1

2

3.6.9.
The Open Aquarium

The introduction in modern aquaristics of hanging lamps, has been accompanied by a renaissance of the »open aquarium«. A century ago aquariums were placed in living rooms, primarily near a window and day light was the only light source. Cyprus grass, North American Saururus and Sagittaria grew out of the aquarium and *Nymphaea* and *Nymphoida* such *N. humboldtiana* grew on the water surface. (5)

Aquarium covers with fluorescent lamps then prevented many swimming and marsh plants and their flowers from being used in the aquarium. The aquarium could not be seen into from above and became a see through fish tank.

The rediscovery of the »open aquarium« has brought aquarium life into the family. All family members, including house pets, can now get closer to the aquarium, look into it from above, and become more aware of the growing and blossoming of anything that comes above the water surface.

Also, those important daily activities such as feeding of the fish, fertilization, water changes and control observations are now much easier. We should also like to mention another advantage of the open aquarium, and that is that the living climate outside of the aquarium is improved by the greater vaporization of the aquarium water. Disadvantages in heated rooms have not been observed. More frequent

4

water change prevents any possible increase in mineral salts content.

1 The open aquarium makes it possible to use once more plants that for a long time were not. For instance the species-rich floating plants. Many are pretty to look at. Besides Linse and Lemna species, there are others well suited for aquarium use. The photo below shows such floating plants: Limnobium laevigatum, Salvinia, Wolffia arrihiza, the smallest flowering plant in the world.

3

5

3.6.10.
Plant Diseases

Plants are living organisms, with very complex function and metabolic structure. We should therefore not be surprised that not only humans and decorative fish can become sick, but plants can as well.

Fortunately, pathologically caused diseases such as plant epidemics caused by viruses, or bacteria, hardly ever occur in the aquarium. Rotten leaves occasionally hold increased amounts of bacteria, this is not the cause but generally the results of plant damage.

Diseased and rotting plants, or partial damages to leaves, such as holes, discolorations and fringing are usually the result either of water chemistry (for example too high pH because of a high bicarbonate content) or diseases caused by a lack, or oversupply, of nutrients.

In making a diagnosis the Aquarist should also check whether the damage could not have been caused by nibbling on the part of snails or fish. It has happened that upon looking a second time with a magnifying glass, the surface of an Echinodorus leaf had been finally grated by a sucking catfish, and had consequently become partially yellow and brown.

Many plant diseases can be prevented by good aquarium practices as suggested in this book, i.e. regular water changes and a well balanced and complete fertilization of the fresh water used. Or the Aquarist should regularly check the plants in his aquarium.

Various factors in the tap water, the strength and color of light, or in the supply of carbon and fish, can have a negative effect on the environmental conditions of the plants. Sometimes the type of growth problem will point to its cause, the lack or oversupply of some nutrient element must be recognised as such a lack may lead to stunted growth, and serious plant damage.

Here again, we can make a comparison with a car. If the motor does not get any fuel, it won't go. But after the tank is filled it works again immediately. If however, during driving, motor oil runs out this can lead to serious motor damage which cannot be corrected.

1 Typical iron defficiency in Echinodorus maior. The leaf and leaf nerves are white or yellow, leaf texture is glassy.
2 Nutrient defficiency in Cryptocorynes. The typical shape of the leaf comes about in non-aquatic plants due to a lack of molybdene. Also in the aquarium defficiencies can occur when one does not use a complete fertiliser.
3 Chlorose in Echinodorus bleheri, the leaf veins however are green. This indicates a defficiency, not iron but perhaps manganese, or possibly too much nitrogen.
4 From bottom to top: increasing damage due to iron over fertilisation (Fetrelon) resulting in ironphosphate deposits, which lead to loss of the plant.
5 The so-called »Christmas Tree« disease in Echinodorus horizontalis. Indicates manganese defficiency, but can also occur due to iron overdosing.
6 Iron overdosing damage in Cryptocoryne wendtii.

117

A lack of carbon for example, has a stunting effect on the growth of many plants. Often this lack is combined with pH that is too high. *Cabomba*, *Hygrophila* and *Alternanthera* particularly react in this manner. In Chapter 3.4.4. we discussed the connection between a lack of carbon dioxide and the pH value in great detail.

In the case of a lack of iron, the plants become yellow and glassy, and finally they die. A typical sign of this is the yellowing of the leaf fiber and leaf nerves. In contrast, when other parts of the leaf become yellow and the nerves remain green, this does not point to a lack of iron, but to a lack of manganese in »Christmas tree sickness«. In this case there is not a real lack, but usually a so called »hidden lack«. Manganese is only needed in traces. Furthermore, these symptoms of a lack can only be observed when certain »competing« nutrients are present in an unbalanced ratio. In the case of manganese, an oversupply of iron can expel the manganese. This sort of situation occurs easily in the aquarium if fertilization is undertaken only with iron preparations.

1

2

3

4

5

6

In this way unused iron accumulates, and is added to the new iron, so that an iron oversupply results.

Oversupplies of iron expel not only manganese and other trace elements in the plants, but iron also reacts chemically with one of the most important plant nutrients, phosphorous. These chemical reactions which lead to iron phosphate precipitation do not occur in the water, but in the plant itself. This is visible in the brown and black leaf discoloration of many aquarium plants. Usually followed shortly thereafter by the disintegration of the plant itself. Thus we recommend that plant fertilization with a tested basic fertilizer only take place, when the water is changed and that the critical nutrients be provided daily with a 24 hour fertilizer.

In aquaristic literature and discussion, it is often said that there are certain aquarium plants which have a negative effect on each other. An example is the supposed antagonism between Cryptocorynes and Vallisneria, the secretions and other effects of which supposedly have a negative effect on one another.

We should like to be quite clear here in saying that there is no such direct mutual effect. However, certain plants are able to actively change the water conditions so that other plants which compete with them suffer, or cannot continue to grow.

7

---

1 Fringed holes in a leaf of Echinodorus as a result of damage done by Ancistrus fish.
2 Brown deposits on leaves of Cryptocorynes. In water with a high carbonate hardness, but not enough CO_2 such damage will occur. This can lead to loss of the plant.
3 This is not the result of a defficiency but damage done by snails.
4 Typical photograh is Cryptocoryne rot.
5 Infra red photography can show plant disease in its early stages. Here a healthy leaf.
6 Although the leaf shows no exterior damage, infrared photography shows that the vein connections are damaged due to nutrient defficiencies.
7 Cryptocoryne walkeri in good healthy condition.
8 Cryptocoryne walkeri attacked by Cryptocoryne rot.

8

To explain this phenomenon, let us consider the following situation which can easily be reconstructed in the aquarium. *Cabomba* and *Egeria* satisfy their need for carbon primarily from the free carbon dioxide in the water. If this is exhausted, Egeria can use the bonded carbon in carbonates. Through this process biogienic decalcification with a corresponding rise in pH to well over 9 occurs in the aquarium. Cabomba is then at a disadvantage since it cannot flourish at a pH over 7.5. (pH barrier). Thus in a competition for the necessary carbon, Cabomba cannot compete with Egeria because Egeria is able to impair the water conditions for Cabomba.

This case will not occur in a well managed aquarium, since here the carbon and pH conditions for both plants remain in the tolerable zone by means of CO_2 fertilization and thus they can grow well next to each other.

1

1 *Cabomba piauhyensis is a very pretentious plant from Central and South America. When however correct light, fertiliser and CO_2 are provided this plant becomes beautiful.*

3.6.11.
Plants as Consumers of Nitrate

Unfortunately we are still relatively helpless in the face of one aquaristic problem, and that is an over supply of nitrate. Nitrate is the highest oxidized form of nitrogen. Nitrate values of 50, 100, 250 milligrams per liter and even much more are sometimes measured in aquariums. Nitrate is present in many tap waters, in large amounts. Furthermore, it is additionally produced through the waste products of fish and their food. The Aquarist can easile measure nitrate levels with a nitrate test.

We know of a number of plants which accept nitrate as nitrogen and are able to use it, but on the other hand we also know of some aquarium plants, such as many types of cryptocorynes, for which nitrate is useless.

In general, nitrogen is needed by plants as ammonium. If they receive nitrate, they must reduce it to ammonium. This is chemical work. Since, however, many cryptocorynes have native waters in which nitrogen is present in the form of ammonium they have not learned how to convert nitrate into ammonium.

In the aquarium cryptocorynes are confronted with large supplies of nitrate which they do not recognize. Since they cannot differentiate in their intake of nutrients, the nitrate is taken in by the plant in large amounts but is then stored in the tissue as »useless«.

Overfertilization with nitrate for example, is considered to be one of the major causes of cryptocoryne rot. For these plants, the smallest chemical or physical change in their environment can have catastrophic effects. Such effects can be caused by sudden changes in light or by chemical additives. However, irregularly provided fertilizers, sudden changes in the CO_2 supply, uncontrolled iron fertilization and water change occurring at too great intervals, can also cause these dismal results. The measures described will lead to the breakdown and reconstruction of the nitrate stored in the plants during the plants metabolic processes.

These and similar treatments, result in the occurrence of toxic intermediate compounds of nitrogen, which attack single leaves as well as entire plants, and consequently cause typical cryptocoryne rot.

---

1 Red or redbrown aquarium plants are excellent to bring contrast to the all green plant background. This is particularly so for the Ammania gracilis (1) and the group of plants shown below consisting of Alternanthera »lilacina«. Both are very good choices. Both however require a lot of light.

1

2

3.7.
Algae

It is almost impossible to arm oneself against algae. Spores of many algae are only a few micrometers large. (One micrometer is equal to 1 one thousandth of millimeter.) They often enter the aquarium when fish and plants are moved or introduced into the aquarium, but they may also enter when the water is changed. Unfortunately, one must always presume that in any aquarium there are a number of algae, which although invisible, are only waiting for suitable conditions, in which to reproduce themselves explosively.

In addition, in the last few years, many tropical algae have been introduced into the aquarium through the increasing fish and plant export from tropical, primarily Asiatic, countries. These algae have found excellent living conditions in native temperatures in our aquariums.

The best protection against algae is to prevent the development of an »algae milieu«. For this reason we made the suggestion in Chapter 3.6.7., that the aquarium should be planted densely from the very beginning with fast growing plants, so that the critical initial phase of the aquarium may also be run-in as quickly as possible. When large amounts of algae occur in the aquarium, this is a sure sign that there is something wrong with the aquarium system. Conversely, an aquarium which is well planted, and in which the plants are growing strongly, there will hardly ever be an algae plague.

However, this is often not the case in practice, and there are enough cases in which the continual annoyance of algae has destroyed the pleasure of keeping an aquarium.

One of the first measures to fight algae should be to learn more about algae and how it relates to plants. First of all, it should be noted that algae are also water plants, which are more simply constructed than the other plants in the aquarium. In principal, though, both types of plants have the same needs for light, temperature and nutrients. There are of course, small differences which decide in the end whether the aquarium environment is suitable for plants or friendly to algae.

Because of the similar existence needs, plants and algae are to be understood as competitors for nutrients. On the other hand it would be wrong to consider algae as parasites, because they compete with the plants only for nutrition and space.

In this book we have consciously conceived of and described an aquarium with the most optimal pre-requisites possible. For if, e.g., the living conditions of the plants are impaired in only one regard, or if the nutrient supply ceases to be balanced, the plant will react immediately with stunted growth. This is when algae take over. They begin to reproduce spontaneously, and now have the advantage over the higher plants.

The greatest algae danger, and a particularly critical situation, can occur shortly after the aquarium has been set-up, since the system in the aquarium is still in the building phase, and the biological rhythm does not yet function perfectly. At this time, the newly planted plants must first grow roots and start to grow. They do not yet assimilate sufficiently, and are therefore not yet completely able to sustain life.

3.7.1.
Blue Algae

The development of Blue algae is particularly likely to occur in this initial phase. Blue algae are particularly dangerous because they grow very quickly and can cause the plants, which are not yet fully able to sustain life, to asphyxiate beneath a greasy veil. These skin-like coats which are often termed »Smear algae«, are mostly blue green in color though sometimes also blackish, purple or brown. At first, one should try to remove them mechanically, although this will never be entirely possible, because even the smallest remnants can grow very quickly into large amounts of algae again.

Unfortunately, there are no known fish or snails which can be used for a »biologic cure« against Blue algae. If it is not possible to cut down the Blue algae plague by removing them, chemicals are available on

the market to provide quick emergency help. See also our remarks in Chapter 3.7.6. – »Emergency Break« against Algae.

3.7.2.
Red Algae

Along with the Blue algae, there are hardly any algae more destructive in the aquarium, than the so called beard, brush, and fir algae, which belong to the Red algae group. These type of algae can attack plants, stones and pieces of wood en masse. The Beard algae are densely growing threads, which mainly attack the borders of leaves and stems. The Brush algae appear as dense bushes on leaves, roots and stones. They are even able to grow like a lawn.

These algae all have the same dark dirty green color. The red color is covered, but becomes visible if the threads of algae are placed in alcohol. To fight these algae, we fortunately have a helper among the aquarium fish. *Epalzeorhynchus siamensis* is particularly destructive to beard algae, provided that it is not spoiled with too many other delicacies.

Here too, we must point out that the use of chemicals to fight algae only makes sense if it simultaneously represents a plant-friendly improvement.

1 *Tufts of green algae can under certain circumstances look attractive. In general however they are undesirable guests in the aquarium. Combatting them is often difficult, as all chemical remedies attack plants as well.*
2 *Red algae, to which the algae shown also belong, can be combatted with algae-eating fish.*
3 *(next page) Smear algae, visible as a brown cover in the aquarium in a macro-shot.*

3.7.3.
Brown Silicic Algae

Brown algae hardly ever occur as a plague in the aquarium, in the way that blue beard and brush algae can. When they do, they appear as a greasy brown film and are rarely thread like. One of the most common reasons for their occurrence is poor lighting and resultant poor assimilation on the part of the plants. Low amounts of oxygen in the water also promote the growth of this type of algae. If the amount of light in the aquarium is improved these algae usually disappear again after a short time.

3.7.4.
Green Algae

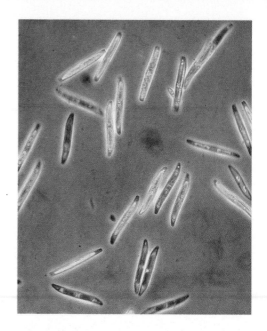

Green algae rarely become a plague in the aquarium. They are most like the higher plants in their existence needs. They can be recognized by their clearly green and usually even light green color. They are closest to the higher plants in their existence needs. They can be recognized by their green, largely light green, color. They can easily be removed by hand or with the correct implement because they are either cotton like, thread like, or bush like in form.

3.7.5.
Fish against Algae

One preventive measure which can be taken against algae, when an aquarium is being set up, is to fill it with algae-eating fish. There are various types which are particularly good at reducing algae. In the following chapters we will meet some of these algae consumers, which can help the Aquarist in his efforts towards an aquarium free of algae. Furthermore we should like to acquaint the reader with an article in Volume 3, 1983, of »Today's Aquarium« in which the entire spectrum of algae eating fish is presented.

3.7.6.
Emergency Break for Algae

If however, blue or green algae have grown to plague dimensions in the aquarium, then the aquarist must use chemical methods to fight algae as a short term measure. But one should be careful here. One must take into account that these chemicals, depending on their concentration, can be damaging, not only to algae, but also to other aquarium plants. Characteristically, chemicals which are useful against algae will attack the algae in a watered down solution and will only attack the plants in a greater concentration.

When using such algicides it is important to follow exactly the instructions for use so that only the prescribed concentration is used.

The success of all measures to fight algae, depends in the last analysis, on whether the aquarist has been successful in making the plant growth active again, by means of water changes and corresponding fresh water preparations, thus making the aquarium system immune to algae again.

These fish are used with differing results to combat algae
1 Poecilia sphenops (Veil-tail molly)
2 Gyrinocheilus aymonieri
3 Ancistrus dolichopterus (Blue Antenna Catfish)
4 Epalzeorhynchus siamensis

3.7.7.

An Ounce of Prevention is worth a Pound of Cure

In this book we have pointed out time and again that optimum plant growth is the best prevention against algae. Plants are the natural competitors for nutrients, however, the completely different structure of an aquarium contains a danger of algae which is often overlooked but can easily occur. This occurs because of too much phosphate. Together with high amounts of nitrate, this makes for a particularly nutritious soil for many algae.

In the aquarium the release of wastes can lead to phosphate contents of five to ten milligrams per liter. (In natural tropical plant waters, we measured PO_4 values between .01 to 1 milligram per liter.)

Even if no plant damage is known to occur on account of too high a phosphate concentration, in the aquarium there is the danger of the development of algae. Algae blooms, blue algae, beard and brush algae, are all unwelcome lovers of phosphor.

Regular PO_4 mesurements will warn of the existence of this danger in time. The preventive measures, which should be taken are a water change, and the planting of fast growing plants.

Two »open aquariums« photographed in an Australian »office«. The tanks have modern hanging lights. The aquarium instrumentation is contained in the cabinet below and the trickle filter in the cabinets next to the aquariums. The plant choice is limited in Australia. Many plants such as Elodea canadensis, E. densa, Alternanthera and Sagettaria sp. can not be cultivated.

1

3.8.
Fish and Food

What we have to say in this chapter about fish is not intended as a complete presentation of tropical fish types, which are suitable for the aquarium. There are numerous good books about fish which can present the reader with a large selection of fish which are suitable for the Optimum Aquarium. In our bibliography you will find some suggestions. It is not the intention of this book to make community tank suggestions. We see our duty as simply to acquaint the reader with things which he must know in order to support, rather than distrub, the system of the optimum aquarium.

This is also true of the food, for it is certainly not interesting for the reader to learn here about complicated living food cultures, since they have no effect on the success of the aquarium system.

3.8.1.
Fish

We aim for an aquarium which offers plants as well as fish optimum living conditions; in which the plants and fish constitute a harmonious unit. This is entirely in our objective. In the fish community to which we have access, we find fish which support our system, and partially even help to make it possible, as well as fish which disturb, or even destroy this system.

As we mentioned in the preceding chapters, the aquarium is particularly sensitive during the initial period, directly after set-up and planting, which means that the water, plants, light, soil, water movement, filtration and heating are factors which function satisfactory over a period of time, before order and the desired stability is archieved, i.e. the true functioning of an artificial biotope.

Naturally, the above mentioned factors are partially able to promote the growth of

---

1 *Otocinclus vittatus*

1

algae, at the beginning, during this period of instability. We know that there are algae in every aquarium, no matter how sterile it has been set up. However, we must try to guarantee the availability of intensive growth factors for the plants on the one hand, and on the other hand we must control the growth of algae. If the plants grow intensively, they can also defend themselves against algae. However, our program does not function as perfectly as in nature, without a helping hand from fish. Since we know some types of fish which in nature prefer to eat algae, we must use them here.

1

Loved aquarium fish:
1 *Colisa lalia, var. red*
2 *Barbus tetrazona*
3 *Plecostomus punctatus*
4 *Colisa lalia, male, wild form*
5 *Hemigrammus sp.*
6 *A school of Petitella georgiae*

2

3

Fish which have up to now been know to prefer to eat algae such as *Gyrinocheilus aymonieri, Otocinclus vittatus, Plecostomus punctatus,* have today been replaced by fish that are much more suitable for the assignment. For a biological algae prevention with fish, we should like to make the following suggestion with the example of a 200 liter aquarium: Algae prevention for Blue and Thread Algae: 6 *Epalzeorhynchos siamensis,* 6 *Poecilia sphenops* (Black Molly). Algae prevention against all algae which colonize decoration material, especially on wood: 2 *Ancistrus dolichopterus.*

In the case of the *Ancistrus dolichopterus* we must note the following reservation: in nature this fish likes to eat cellulose. For this reason it is necessary to add pine resin wood, which it can eat completely clean, in addition to the algae which it desires. Otherwise it can easily happen that this fish will take the harder plant leaves, for example, leaves of *Echinodorus* types as algae pasture. In the course of grazing, it can easily harm the epidermis, and the leaf will begin to rot. In our experience these three fish types have worked very well, and have kept the growth of algae in a newly established aquarium under control. They ought to be placed in the aquarium immediately after the planting, simultaneously with a suitable water preparation or peat filtration.

Certainly you will ask yourself, why we do not recommend fish such as *Gyrinocheilus aymonieri, Otocinclus vittatus* and *Plecostomus punctatus,* which were mentioned above. We do not, because these three fish have the following disadvantages:

1. *Gyrinocheilus aymonieri* is good for consuming algae as long as it is young, and does not get any additional food. As soon as it becomes larger, it also becomes lazy, and vicious towards other aquarium inhabitants.
2. *Otocinclus vittatus* is a very shy fish, and is easily disturbed during feeding by other inhabitants. Furthermore it is too sensitive for our purposes, and not effective enough in algae consumption.
3. *Plecostomus punctatus* grows up to 30 centimeters in nature and changes the amazome sword plants into lattice plants.

4

5

6

Should the reader ask why we recommend so many algae consumers for a 200 liter aquarium, we should like to point out that the algae eating fish recommended here lives in large communities in nature. If placed individually in the aquarium they often lose their uniqueness. If however, they are placed in small schools in the aquarium they are much more active, and productive on account of their feeding habits.

During the initial phase, until the regular stock has been placed in the aquarium, the algae eaters should not receive any additional food. It is in no way harmful if they have to go a little hungry in the first stages, because obviously not enough algae are present. On the contrary, with these apparently rash measures, we are teaching them to fulfill their function as trained algae eaters over the long term.

Along with these fish which actively support the functioning of the Optimum Aquarium, there are of course other fish which can be severely destructive to our system. We should like to point out again that we are not concerned with the special aquarium (Discus breeding aquarium,

1 Ottocinclus affenis, the smallest of the Ottocinclus varieties. All Ottocinclus types except the one on page 127 O. vittatus are good algae-eaters.
2 Pterophyllum altum (real scalare) is only to be used in larger aquaria.

1 *Julidochromis ornatus*
2 *Tetraodon palembangensis*, an excellent snail eater.

colorful perch aquarium, or goldfish aquarium) but with a tropical community aquarium in which fish and plants should live together harmoniously. One of these disturbers of the peace is *Anostomus anostomus,* which specializes in nibbling on our fine plants tirelessly. *Metynnis hypsauchen* is a fish which can only be nourished with lettuce leaves or water plants, and which therefore is automatically disqualified from our aquarium. *Cichlasoma meeki* are a very attractive fish to breed, but is not suitable for the aquarium because of its agitation.

Many other fish belong in this category, such as the African colorful perch of the Pseudo-tropheus type, which with its scraper snout nourishes itself in nature with algae and plants, and because of its natural environment also prefers an alkali pH. These fish too are enemies of water plants.

At this point we should like to point out that there are many colorful and very peaceful types of African perch, which do not eat at the water plants, nor do they stir up the substrate. These are for example *Julidochromis marlieri* and *Julidochromis ornatus*. *Acanthophthalmus kuhli* gets on well with plants but has the unpleasant characteristic of burrowing in the substrate at night. Unfortunately, usually in places where the delicate water plants grow. Thailand Thorn Eels (*Mastacembelus aculeatus*) have the

same characteristics. The Hai Barbe (*Balantiocheilus melanopterus*) however, is a fish which likes to nibble on the fine points of many water plants.

Botia macracantha and the *Labeo bicolor* are loaches which tend to up-set the decorative arrangement of our water plants, because of their inconsistent behavior in the aquarium, particularly when they have a chance to develop their ideosyncrasies, and thus are present in a school. They like to burrow and can really disturb the aquarium decoration.

The group of goldfish and vail tail of the *Carassius* family, are also unsuitable for our aquarium for two reasons:
1. They are uncomfortable in the tropical temperatures between 25 and 26° C in our aquarium.
2. As a secondary food source they like to nibble on sweet water plants.

Puffer fish in general, such as the leopord or the Figure Puffer fish, which we normally only place in the aquarium in order to take care of the snails, and then only for a short time, can be antagonists of water plants, because they bite large circular holes in the plant leaves.

The *Monodactylus argenteus* and the *Scatophagus argus rubrifrons* should be mentioned since these two fish come from pure sea water or from river water mixed with sea water, and thus do not feel well in our aquarium without additional salt. If however we want to add salt our plants won't grow. These fish which in nature feed on algae and also on plants are thus not suitable for our aquarium.

Naturally, we do not intend this list to have been complete. In this case we can only point to more detailed literature, which has the function of describing more in detail, and more clearly, the requirements of such fish. We want to make sure only that when setting up a system aquarium with fish, the Aquarist pays attention to their requirements. If one of your favorite fish has been left off the list, please be consoled with the fact that there are more than a thousand different types of fish at your disposal, and there are countless ways in which our fish community, which is pleasant for both us and for the plants, can be put together. To make a suggestion concerning that community at this point would be presumptuous, since this is usually entirely a matter of taste. However, at this point we should like to give some tips which may make your choice easier:

1. There are antagonists among fish too. i.e. one fish may eat or at least nibble at another.
2. The number of fish of each family should be on the high side, i.e. a school of neon fish, of 10 to 20 fish, in a 100 liter aquarium is much more pleasurable to the eye, than a confusion of 20 different types.
3. The size of the fish, when they are fully grown, should be in harmony with the aquarium architecture, i.e. a large Scalare in a 35 centimeter high aquarium certainly does not look very good.
4. It must be kept in mind that fish are generally young and not fully grown when they are bought, and that with good care in our system aquarium they will quickly reach their natural size.
5. It is superfluous to mention that the temperature needs of the fish must be in harmony with the plants.
6. A good rule to follow is one centimeter fish to two liters of water. (2/3 inch per gallon)

1 *Corydoras hastatus, the smallest of the Corydoras types*
2 *Apistogramma ramirezi (Ram)*
3 *Pelvicachromis pulcher, a pair with fry, example of a fish parent family*
4 *Colisa lalia, red, at the height of spawning*
5 *A nice school of Micralestes interruptus*

4

5

3.8.2.
Feeding the Aquarium Fish

The feeding of tropical fish in the aquarium should be as optimal as providing aquarium plants with light, carbonic acid, the necessary nutrients, and trace elements. The Aquarist who wishes to possess an Optimum Aquarium takes on the responsibility of feeding the lives which have been entrusted to him, i.e. the fish for which he is caring, in a way which is both biologically correct and appropriate for the types of fish.

The basic question is what sort of fish food should be used? Is it at all possible to correctly feed a variety of fish, with very different biological structure, when it comes to nutrition, as is often the case in an aquarium, with a single type of food?

In this chapter we want to attempt to provide some satisfactory solutions. Let us first consider what our fish eat in their tropical environment.

3.8.3.
What do the Fish eat in Nature

Professor Dr. Rolf Geisler an ichthiologist and a true specialist in tropical water, published in Today's Aquarium a series of articles, concerning the correct feeding of aquarium fish. We should like to quote from these articles. Although there are still gaps in the scientific literature on the nutrition biology of small tropical fish, the foundations are quite clear. Thus, while in nature the fish enjoy a wide selection of natural food, at least at times, in the aquarium they receive rather simple and monotonous food.

However, it is also not the case that the fish, in their native waters, swim into a supply of food for the entire year. After a period of abundance of food, there are also periods in which the fish must go hungry. This is an important law of nature.

Particularly indicative, although dated, are the fundamental studies by Professor Rudolf Braun at the so called River Lakes of Rio Tapajoz in tropical Brazil. Here Geisler later found large numbers of *Pterophyllum*, *Apistogramma*, *Crenicara* and smaller salmon. On page 136 is a graphical summary of Brown's findings concerning the seasonal changes in the available nutrition. According to his findings, at the beginning of the rainy period, and the resulting rising water, an ever increasing amount of animal plankton grows, and there are also greater amounts of white mosquito larvae and soil animals, in the main mosquito larvae. At the same time, the spawning period of most types of fish begins. This observation is interesting since, where there is a decreasing or completely lacking supply of red mosquito larvae, there is an increasing amount of white mosquito larvae. The plankton rich period is also the period in which the fish fry go through their critical youth phase. At Rio Tapajoz the months of September to November, the so called dry period, in which there was little precipitation, were hunger months for the fish. Thus, the nutrition supply is greatly affected by the dry period and the rainy period, by rising and falling water.

When the water is rising many of the jungle trees, in and around the water, bloom and bear fruit. Fruits and seeds are then eaten by the salmon. Hatchet fish chase bloom dust. Salmon such as *Leporinus* eat fresh water sponges. Airborne food, such as small insects, are sought the entire year long by many types of fish. Thus the meal plan in tropical nature is very varied not only in choice, but also in amount.

1 Underwater photo of a large aquarium, through the front pane. Epalzeorhinchus siamensis eating food tablets, which interferes with their algae-eating habits.

3.8.4.
Live Food

Considering the meal plan of fish in nature, it is relevant to ask how live food can be provided in the aquarium. There are three major problems here: acquisition, quality and time spent.

Let us not consider the latter problem. Every Aquarist must decide for himself how much time he wishes to spend acquiring live food.

Good live food is without a doubt the best for optimal fish care, and fish breeding. Unfortunately finding the pond of yesteryear has become very difficult. A large amount of tubifex and red mosquito larvae, for example, is dependent on flowing water loaded with organic waste products. Since today, not only easily dissolved and septic waste waters are drained away, but also materials such as heavy metals and Chlor hydro carbons, which are difficult or even impossible to break down, this brings about the danger that the two live foods mentioned above, contain these dangerous materials, which then are taken in by the fish.

The situation is considerably better in the case of pools and ponds in which there are plenty of water fleas and Cyclops. These animals are indicators of good water, and are very valuable live food for fish fry, and the smaller types of fish. The danger that parasites causing disease, found in the natural waters will be brought into the aquarium, is according to our experience, exaggerated.

However, fresh water hydra which can easily be brought into the aquarium along with live food, can be really very troublesome.

To sum up, the best live food should be taken from standing water which does not contain fish. The food should then be left in a bucket for a number of hours so that the hydra can settle. Even the smallest food pond in one's own garden can be a great help in optimizing fish feeding.

Countless food animals can be bred in the home. These include slipper animalcules, artemia, grindal worms, Enchytraes and rain worms. There is plenty of specific literature on this subject. Black mosquito

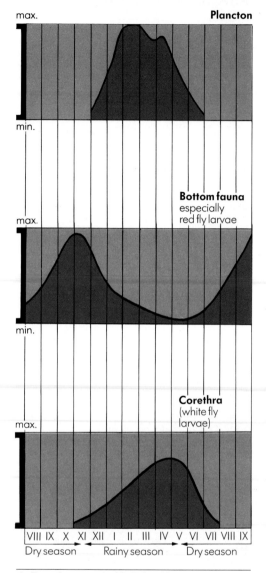

1 Development of fish food in waters in the Rio Tapajos (Brazil) Schematic based on measurements by R. Braun.

larvae which are practically indispensable in breeding some types of fish, can be easily bred between April and October, in the garden or on the balcony. Any open tub in which an old perlon stocking, filled with fresh grass, can be placed is sufficient. The small mosquito larvae can easily be fished out before they become mosquito's.

Brine shrimp, *Artemia salina*, is particularly valuable food, biologically. With a little know-how the nauplii can be used to feed the fish fry, and the brine themselves are valuable food for larger fish. The great nutritional-physiological value of artemia is documented by the experience that artemia have never been able to be replaced as fry food, or food for fish such as carp, by other raw materials.

---

1 A pair of Cichlasoma sajica. Even in their normal coloring these fish are beautiful. The female can be recognised from the goldtone in the fins.

3.8.5.
Frozen Food

Some of the most important food animals, such as the red, white and black mosquito larvae, water fleas, cyclops, mysis and others are available to the Aquarist as deep-frozen food, which is particularly helpful in the winter. It can happen that in the case of red mosquito larvae, that there may still be remains of dangerous elements in the larvae. There is unfortunately no brand name product, which the manufacturer guarantees with his knowledge and his name.

So called freeze-dried food, mostly red mosquito larvae, but some tubifex as well, provides many fish with excellent food. There are some very good quality foods on the market, largely ash free and without particles.

1

3.8.6.
Dry Food

We need not go into our feelings any further, about the claim »dry food for all tropical decorative fish«, but no matter how you look at it, more than 90 % of all Aquarists do need dry food or more specifically, mixed dry food.

The quality of such food is relatively high, although it could be further developed. Today's Hobby would not be spread over the entire world, would such dry food not be available. Thus, our concern is not with the raw materials used, but with the poor supply of fresh products on the market. If stored too long, particularly in warm rooms, at high levels of humidity, raw materials, such as fats, can change for the worse and vitamins which were present upon manufacturing, or which were added at that time, may no longer be present in the quantity needed.

The optimal mixed dry food will have the following:

1. Informative data on the package
2. Low fat content
3. Vitamin content stability until usage.
4. Full information on preservatives used.
5. Full information on artificial colors used.

1. Informative data.
Of course the Aquarist expects that raw materials of only the highest quality were used, in preparing the food. Manufacturers are not required to state clearly the contents of pet foods, which includes food for aquarium fish; and objective information in advertising is limited. The Aquarist who is thirsty for knowledge, and wants to achieve optimal feeding should be able to tell what the basic components of the dry food are. For example, what is the protein content? There are, for example, countless animal and plant proteins, but their digestibility is quite different.

It is particularly important for the breeder to know how much digestible protein is contained in the food. Breeding fish should be fed considerably less protein than other fish and fry. The information offered by some manufacturers is limited, indeed almost pitiful. What does the following information mean, for example: At least

43 % protein. What is the upper limit? Food for decorative fish must be judged differently from dry food for staple fish, as in this case the only important consideration is that they grow quickly and economically. In short, more information is urgently needed.

2. Fat content.
Aquarium fish get much less exercise than fish in the natural environment. Thus their need for fat in their food is quite law. Too much fat can easily lead to liver damage, and can also damage the gonads. There is a saying »a good rooster rarely becomes fat«.

The use of fat is very dependent on temperature. However in heating the aquarium, many Aquarists try to save on electricity. It would be desirable to have more information concerning fat content in the various products, as opposed to such generalizations as »manufactured from the best raw materials«.

3. Vitamins.
Depending on the manufacturing process, vitamins may be lost during drying, which can be compensated for by corresponding additions of vitamins. Further loss of certain vitamins will occur depending on the raw materials used, the length and type of storage, the packaging and the room temperature, as well as on the amount of time between manufacturing and use. For this reason, food for edable fish, such as trout and carp, must legally indicate a date by which the food must be used on the package. Manufacturers of dry food for aquarium fish however, are silent on this point.

4. Preservatives.
In order to halt mycrobial enzymatic decomposition, and vitamin loss in ready-made food, so called anti-oxydants are added to the dry food. Chemical preservatives are often necessary, but the Aquarist should be aware of their existence. The fewer the preservatives, the better.

5. Artificial coloring.
What is the advantage in terms of optimal fish nutrition? If an initially homogenous mixture is then colored brown, red and green the fish don't care, but it does give the Aquarist the impression of variety, which in fact does not exist. The en-

lightened Aquarist can do without artificial coloring in the fish food. Or do you too buy »by sight«?

Summary

This list points out problems with dry food, and in addition explains why well known breeders of decorative fish are skeptical concerning feeding exclusively with dry food. Problems are however solvable, only a little at a time. In the future dry food will continue to be the basic source of nutrition for aquarium fish. However we do recommend that the Aquarist avoid monotony and in addition to the basic food, also provides the fish with live food, and as a replacement frozen food, according to the type of fish. We are all aware of what kind of nutrition is best for humans. The same is true of aquarium fish.

1

3.8.7.
Feeding

In aquaristic practice, dry food should be used as follows:
1. Two or three times a day give only as much food as is eaten up within a few minutes.
2. If there are new fish in the aquarium it is recommended that a fifth of the necessary food be provided five times a day, since this type of feeding increases the desire to eat on the part of the fish, however, one should remember that the amount of dry food expands greatly in water.
3. When different fish are being fed, keep their different eating habits in mind, for example, Cichlids prefer cichlid flakes, Cat fish prefer round tablets.
4. It is therefore advisable to use more than one type of food and to provide as much variety as possible in types of food.

Keep in mind that many fish suffer under the feeding desires of those who keep them. Generally we give our decorative fish too much food. As we have mentioned before, dry food expands in water, so the volume of food once in the water, is considerably larger than what one originally had in ones hand. Don't worry if your fish don't appear to be particularly hungry, especially at the beginning. During this phase they are probably having difficulties getting used to the environment. After about 14 days at the most however, they will have acclimatized themselves. You will not be able to awaken the fishes desire to eat by giving them more food. Small portions are always better.

One more tip. Algae occur easily if too much food is given. By means of a phosphate measurement you can tell if the algae are building, and can then correct the feeding habits if the phosphate content is rising, or if necessary you can reduce the number of fish. An increasing amount of nitrate also shows how well your aquarium system is dealing with the amount of food. The most elegant method of correcting the situation is to change up to 20 to 30 % of the water at regular intervals.

Don't forget that it is necessary to add a complete fertilizer in addition to the above measures.

1 *Apistogramma agassizii, a fish which likes both live and dry food.*

3.8.8.
Vacation

If you want to go on vacation, you should take the following steps before you leave, and also if necessary add some instruments onto your aquarium.

● The most important thing to keep in mind is that the fish and plants should have become used to their environment before you go on vacation, and the aquarium should be at least 3 to 4 months old.
● Furthermore, the fish should be nourished well and with good variety, before your vacation.
● Keep in mind that there should be one centimeter of fish to two liters of water.

These are the most important pre-requisites, but we should like to make the following suggestions as well.

● Clean the filter before you go away;
● Change the water and add a complete fertilizer;
● Check the CO_2 apparatus and fill the CO_2 depot bottle.
● Add a light switch timing device, if you don't have one already, and check it again if necessary.
● It is always better to leave the feeding to a machine than to a beloved aunt.
● If there is a nutrient dosing pump present, the storage container should be filled again before you go away.
● If your aquarium has a low heat capacity and you are going away during the winter so that the room temperature will sink considerably below normal, you should probably add a heater to the aquarium.

If you already have a well functioning Optimum Aquarium, you can go away for 3 to 4 weeks without having to feed your fish. Don't worry about hunger periods for in nature your aquarium fish are not used to always having a sufficient supply of food. If you go on vacation you can let your fish fast a little, without worrying.

So called vacation food, or weekend food, which can be given in a single dose, should not be put into the aquarium because these food mixtures cause not only loss of oxygen, a lower pH, rot and algae formation, but in the worst case, the fish themselves can be damaged by this type of food.

1 A couple of Tateurndia ocellicauda pairing. The male closes his fins and lays against the body of the female.

1

3.9.
Lighting

We have already mentioned a number of times how important the correct lighting is for the Optimum Aquarium. So at this point we consider it necessary to deal with this point in greater detail.

Light in nature:
1 90 000 Lux and algae growth
2 90 000 Lux and no algae
3 Only 1 000 Lux and still good plant growth. The sunlight reaches through the leaf covering.
4 100 Lux and still good plant growth. The exceptional about this: all these plants were found in the same habitat.

1

2

3

4

3.9.1.
Strength of Light and Nature

The strength of light, and light temperatures, which we have measured in nature prompt us to correct some classic ideas. For example we found Cryptocorynes, which have always been considered a shade plant, in very sunny as well as very shady places. The difference in Lux was between fifty and ninety thousand Lux. These plants grew in the darkest part of the stream at a point where the depth was 3.5 meters. It would of course be wrong to conclude that an aquarium does not need stronger light and that one can be satisfied with fifty Lux. We may not forget that, in nature, water plants also suffer in certain places, and that leaves falling from and growing on the trees cause great fluctuations in light intensity.

3.9.2.
Light Color Spectrum

A similar situation exists with regard to light color spectrum. There are people who believe that a median day light temperature of 5600 Kelvin degrees should be kept in the aquarium, because this is supposedly the case in nature. Those readers who are also photographers, can confirm that slide film, that is exposed in the early morning or in the afternoon, has quite different colors than if it is exposed at noon.

On the occasion of our regular expeditions we measured the color temperature of tropical light, as well as the number of Lux, and determined that the Kelvin value increased in the early morning hours from 3000 to 3600, 4560 and finally 6000, when the sun reached its highest point. In the afternoon the curve decreased again until the sun went down. Shady places where there are water plants, do not have the color temperature of natural sunlight. The green shimmer of light in these places, which is

1

caused by the leaves has a great effect on the color temperature.

If we apply this knowledge to the aquarium we realize that we should not take too much trouble with light temperature. In choosing the colors of fluorescent lamps, we should consider the following.

● Warm color lamps (about 3600 Kelvin) promote elongated growth. Cold color lamps (about 6000 Kelvin) promote bushy growth. Usually the Lumen values reached with cold color and warm color tubes are the same.
● Furthermore, the desire to see fish and plants in a natural light is justified.
● The light must be strong enough to promote photosynthesis assimilation, and the necessary metabolism. This means that we must achieve a good median value in lighting.

Many of today's aquariums are lighted much too weakly. For example the 80 centimeter standard aquarium is often provided with a 60 centimeter fluorescent lamp and if we measure the lamp we will register only 500 to 1000 Lux on the water surface, and only 20 to 30 Lux on the substrate. This of course is too little.

Light colours (l. to r.) White, Gro-Lux or Fluora, Daylight, Warmlight.

3.9.3.
Type of Lighting

Before we consider the use and economics of the different types of lighting, we should like to clarify how the economics of lamps can be determined. Every lighting source has a certain light flux, which is high, or low, depending on how the light source is built. This light stream is called Lumen. The catalog of any lighting manufacturer contains the Lumen value. The Lumen should always be considered together with the wattage when determining the economics.

For example a forty watt fluorescent lamp has a total Lumen of 3000. If we divide the Lumen by forty watts, we get 75 Lumen per watt. (In the case of a normal fluorescent tube).

If we look at the list of lighting methods below, we discover something very interesting concerning economics. We see that we have a great choice of lighting methods, and can choose the most productive or economical method.

Furthermore in choosing a lighting method, consider how you want to light your aquarium.

It is possible to light the entire aquarium with a long fluorescent tube, while a round lamp such as e.g. a high pressure HQL light, will light only a part of it. Areal-lighting allows even softer lighting of the entire aquarium. Since in this case the light doesn't hit the aquarium with high intensity, the aquarium height is limited when such fluorescent lamps are added on. The maximum depth when using fluorescent tubes is 50 cm (approx. 18 inches).

The aquarium is lighted with more contrast when using directed lighting such as high pressure HQL and metal Halide (HQI) lamps for example. As a result there are areas of strong light and shaded ones. This has some advantages:

A. We achieve a high light intensity in certain areas, which would be impossible with a fluorescent tubes. We also get shaded areas, which the fish like to rest in.

B. Because of the light intensity we can have a water level of up to 80 centimeters, if we use a high pressure lamp for example.

From an economical standpoint things are naturally quite different. Looked at it from this standpoint, the fluorescent lamp will always be preferable.

Now that we are aware of Lumen we should like to recommend 30 to 50 Lumen per liter of water in the Optimum Aquarium.

3.9.3.1.
Fluorescent Lamps

In Chapter 3.2 – Aquarium size, we mentioned that we wanted to limit ourselves to certain aquarium measurements, e.g. 70, 100, 130, and 160 centimeters. We can use the following tubes for these aquariums. Sixty centimeters equals 20 watts. Ninety centimeters equal 30 watts; one hundred and twenty centimeters equal 40 watts and 150 centimeters equal 65 watts. The 10 centimeter difference, is meant for the sockets to the right and left.

In practice this means that an aquarium with the measurements of 130 × 55 × 45 centimeters (approximately 320 liters) must be illuminated with between 117 and 200 watts. Thus to light this aquarium ideally we must provide 3 times 40 = 120 watts, to 5 times 40 = 200 watts. So we are illuminating this aquarium with approximately 10 000 to 17 000 Lumen.

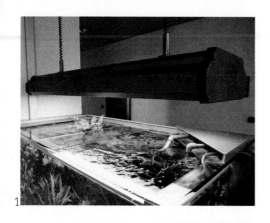

1 *Fluorescent tubes in a modern housing. Several such fluorescent tubes ensure that enough light is available in large aquaria.*

cent of the light energy released is lost in the light casing, because it is not directed downwards. Closed light boxes also known as »strips« have a definite disadvantage in the summer time, when the room temperature goes above 25 degrees Celsius. The operating temperature is so high that we are no longer in control of the aquarium water temperature. Furthermore the life of a fluoresscent lamp depends not only on how often it is turned on and off, but also on operating temperature. Fluorescent lamps become very hot at either end and when an excessive temperature is reached for a length of time, the light capacity of these lamps falls by 50 % in half a year.

Changing fluorescent lamps is always somewhat complicated because of the fact that these lamps are water proof (in Germany). If the Aquarist is unsure or unknowledgeable, someone who works in a pet store will be able to make the change. You must go to the nearest pet store with your lamp in this case.

A good alternative is the free hanging lamps, that are hung directly over the aquarium. The first lamps to be hung were the mercury vapor lamps, which could be hung freely over the aquarium. This technique has the following advantages:

● The lamp doesn't touch the aquarium. This provides the greatest possible safety.
● The operating temperature of these lamps is normal, and doesn't effect the aquarium during the summer, and the lumilux fluorescent lamps life time, is lengthened to at least 12 months.
● Since there is now much more space over the aquarium care is simpler,
● Since we can see into the aquarium from above, we have a continuous overview of events in it.

If a water plant grows towards the light through an opening in the cover, which can be removed in summer, the lamps may be hung higher, perhaps by means of a spiral cord. This will make the aquarium visible by means of lighting, also from the top.

It is not as easy to set up free hanging fluorescent lamps as a lamp unit placed on the aquarium. However, there are three ways to do it.

● Safety spiral cord hanging from the ceiling,
● Corner bracket hanging from the wall or
● Bracket attached to the aquarium itself.

In putting together the tubes we should choose one, or at the most two colors. In our aquariums we have had the best results with light color 11, lumilux daylight and light color 21, lumilux white. This provides a good mixed light that is perfect in color. Initially we do not recommend the true violet plant lamps, (Gro-lux and Fluora) for the Optimum Aquarium, since they have the unpleasant characteristic of promoting the development of blue algae during the running in of the aquarium. Later, after 3 to 6 months, one fluorescent tube can be replaced by a plant lamp.

Now let us consider another problem. When placing the aquarium lighting, keep in mind that all artificial light sources over the aquarium must be water proof, according to the technical directions in force. As a result lamps for aquarium use, have improved considerably and they are also provided with very effective reflectors. (A logical conclusion from the first to the 4th edition of this book.) Lamps that don't have reflectors should be refused, since 30 per-

3.9.3.2.
Mercury Vapor Lamps (HQL)

Mercury vapor lamps are usually hung free over the aquarium. Earlier they were mainly used in industry, and were only discovered for aquaristic use by Aquarists upon the publication of a book entitled »The Perfect Aquarium«, eight years ago. Today there are countless mercury vapor lamps giving between 50 and 250 watts. However, a number of these lamps are not suitable for our use, because their radiation angle is so wide that the light which we want to have in the aquarium goes beyond the measurements of the aquarium. For this reason we should like to present the functions which the mercury vapor lamp must fulfill at any rate.

1. The mercury vapor lamp must have a deep parabolic reflector which gathers the light with the least possible loss, and directs into the aquarium.
2. The mercury vapor lamp should not blind the Aquarist in any way, when he is sitting in an arm chair in front of his aquarium.
3. The housing of the mercury vapor lamp must be rust free (aluminium) so that even the smalles amount of water from the aquarium cannot rust the underside of the lamp.
4. The mercury vapor lamp must be switchable, for example from 80 to 125 watts in order to be able to use less lighting at a later point, after initial good plant growth. In this case, of course, the original 125 watt bulb must be exchanged for an 80 watt bulb.
5. Last but not least, we should like to mention that the mercury vapor lamp should blend in form and color, with the Aquarists' house, and should be in harmony with its environment. The fifty watt mercury vapor lamp has not had much success in the hobby, because it is not economical, and does not bring the desired results.

1 Example of a modern aquarium light, free hanging over an open aquarium (Dupla System). The low heat radiation makes it possible for all plants to grow towards the light.

The 250 watt mercury vapor lamp has been largely replaced by more modern mercury vapors about which we will speak later.

The mercury vapor lamp can be suspended from the ceiling by means of a safety spiral cord or hung from a corner on the wall above the aquarium using a wall bracket. One must keep in mind that one should be able at a later point in time, to change the height of the lamp. At a distance of 20 centimeters over the water surface, 30 000 to 40 000 Lux is achieved with a good 125 watt lamp.

In the first 1978 edition of the book »The Perfect Aquarium« we mentioned that the economies of the mercury vapor lamp were very good, and that the light loss in two years only comes to 20 %. Unfortunately we have to change these remarks since we have discovered that particularly the 80 and 125 watt bulbs which are manufactured by the millions, no longer have this life span. On the average there is a light loss of 20 % in 8 to 12 months. For this reason it's important to make an occasional light measurement.

Any light meter can make this measurement. You will get comparative values by taking a certain predetermined light mix at a certain time and DIN. After half a year, use these same values to take another measurement. If the lighting measure shows a lower mix of light, you can assume that the light source has diminished.

3.9.3.3.
Metal Halide Lamps (HQI)

The Metal Halide Lamp was developed ten years ago for industry. It was primarily used to light gymnasiums and film and television studios with neutral white light. Six years ago Horst E. Kipper used a Metal

1

2

1 + 2 Example of strong and healthy plant growth, using these very modern intensive light fixtures (Dupla System)

Halide Lamp with his 10 000 liter aquarium, and achieved considerable approvement in the aquarium.

The Metal Halide Lamp is available in

various forms, for example, bulb form, eliptic form, tube form, and a tube form with double sided contact. The tube form with double sided contact at 150 watt and 250 watt NDL is already being used in some areas of the hobby with great success. NDL is neutral white, and any daylight slide film shows how correct that light is. The good

economy of about 77 Lumen approaches the economy of fluorescent lamps.

We are unfortunately not yet able to make any statements concerning the light span, but we believe that it approximates a normal Metal Halide Lamp. The information given by the manufacturer concerning its life span always consists of lower values which can be considerably exceeded.

If you use a Metal Halide Lamp for the aquarium look out for the following:
1. The reflector must be so well built that it collects the light equally and sends it into the aquarium without blinding the Aquarist.

1 Respecting the recommended distance between water and light of 40 cm, and using HQI lights (Dupla System) enables the Hydroculture behind the aquarium to receive the proper amount of light.

1

2. Generally the lamp can be hung only with a chain or from a wall bracket since the body of the lamp becomes very hot.
3. The casing should be, if possible, made of aluminium or diecast aluminum because of the danger of corrosion when the lamp is turned off at night.
4. Safety precautions prescribe that every such lamp be provided with, and only be operated when, a safety glass is present.
5. The distance between this high intensity lamp and the aquarium must be at least 40 centimeters (approx 15 inches).

With this high intensity lamp we can illuminate water levels of up to 100 centimeters (250 watt Metal Halide).

3.9.4.
Light Direction

In nature, the yearly average on the sun's rising and setting, is 6:00 in the morning and 6:00 in the evening. So we also light our aquarium for 10 to 12 hours. It has been our experience that more lighting does not have any advantage and a shorter lighting time may be dangerous.

We see from typical night activity that generally, during the 10 to 12 hour dark period, plants such as *Hygrophila* put up their leaves to show that they do not need any more light and are entering a period of non-assimilation. Here we should like to stress that it would be senseless to divide the 12 hour lighting period in 2 or 3 parts of the day. For example, 2 hours when the Aquarist gets up, then again from 12 noon until 6:00 in the evening, and again from 8:00 until midnight. The biorhythm of the entire aquarium would be considerably damaged by this, and there would be no satisfactory plant growth.

It is also true that weak lighting can not be compensated for by lengthening the time of lighting.

In order to avoid mistakes from the very beginning, we recommend urgently that a timing device be installed for every lighting apparatus over the aquarium, which takes care of the regular on and off switching of the light. We know from our experience, that it is useful to turn on the light at 10

1 + 2 Does the »sleep« appearance of these plants indicate that their light requirement for the stay has been satisfied? Certainly an interesting question.

o'clock in the morning, and thus go without the morning view of the aquarium, but thus to be able to observe the aquarium in the evening.

3.10.
Heating

In our inventory in Chapter 2.2. we pointed out that the heating of most contemporary aquariums is faulty because it is either too strong or too weak. We should like to come back to this topic again here.

3.10.1.
Natural Sources of Warmth

Since we have tropical fish and plants in the aquarium, it is necessary to consider the tropical temperature. The water temperature in the tropics fluctuates generally between 24 and 27 degrees Celsius. Of course there are peak temperatures particularly in water puddles and in rice fields of 34 degrees. However, we need not consider these extremes here, since they are only temporary temperatures, and the biotope in these areas exists only for a short time (rainy period, dry period, etc.).

3.10.2.
Heating the Aquarium

As a rule our room temperatures today are between 18 and 21 degrees Celsius, which means that we have a difference of about 4 to 7 degrees between our room temperatures and the tropical aquarium. It also means that we must provide additional heating for our tropical aquarium.

3.10.3.
Heat Performance

Unfortunately, one watt per liter has always been recommended, in order to cope with temperature fluctuations of up to 15 degrees if necessary. However, recent experience has shown that we can do without this great heat capacity. On the contrary we must always deal with problems of overheating, for example, because of an incorrectly ventilated light or too strong heating.

In the Optimum Aquarium we can get along very well with a heating capacity of 0.3 to 0.5 watts per liter of aquarium water.

In comparison to the first edition of this book, which appeared in 1978, we have had to raise the heat norms since the average temperature in houses who use heating oil in Europe, Japan, and America, during the winter, have changed. Because of the rise in price of energy sources we have all become more economical, and many aquarists have reduced the temperature in their living room. For this reason we must raise the heat capacity a little. We must particularly remember that if we go away on vacation during the winter, the heat provided must be raised if the room temperature will decrease considerably (decrease at night, add an additional heater).

It is wrong to think however, that the heat wattage can be increased from the start, in order to cope with the winter and any decrease in room temperature. We stress the importance of limited heating because of continuity i.e. the balanced heating of an aquarium, without warmth peaks, is undoubtedly better and more advantageous.

1 Modern instrument with an accuracy of 0.1°C. Digital indicator can be inserted at a later date. 100 % watertight probes ensure a correct temperature measurement.

We know that continual heating of an aquarium is better than single intense short term heating. Since, generally there are still many aquariums today with bi-metal heat regulators, intensive short term heating is an important factor contributing to the decrease in lifetime of the regulator. In a 24 hour period, for example, with a heat capacity of 1 watt per liter, and a corresponding cooling phase, we can witness intermittent switching of upto twenty times. With a correctly calculated heating of 0.3 to 0.5 watts, however, we register only 50 to 10 intermittent switching impulses. This means that these bi-metal thermostat/regulators work for twice as long a time. One has tobear in mind especially, that in the case of intensive heating (1 watt per liter) the bi-metal regulator can stick, which will then lead to the overheating of the aquarium, and this in turn can cause something of a catastrophe.

One can avoid the disadvantages of the bi-metal regulator by using electronics.

Today there are many electronic regulators on the market which work excellently. Before choosing an electronic regulator one should know something about the different ways in which they work, and what one can demand of a good regulating apparatus. With electronic regulation, a triac can be included which can produce 50 switch impulses in one second without any wear and tear. However, with these triac regulators it is very complicated to eleminate interference, and they can't work with inductive loads on low volt transformers. The triac regulator would destroy any transformer within 5 minutes with switch impulses.

Other regulators work with relays, which switch on and off mechanically. Of course in this case wear and tear occurs, but when you consider that a good electronic relay controlled with lower voltage can switch upto 6 million times, this means that the relay has a life span of between 15 and 20 years.

The preuse measuring quality of these regulators is quite good, thanks to probes and Hysteris. A regulator with an accuracy

1

of + or − 0.1 degrees Celsius is common place. The measuring probe of the temperature sensor should be as long and as water tight as possible, so that it can easily be guided to the aquarium from a lower cupboard.

For security reasons the measuring probe must be provided with low voltage electricity so that the damage to the cable by fish, or sharp edged decorative objects, will not allow dangerous electricity to flow into the aquarium.

The temperature can easily be determined with electronic regulators on a clearly arranged scale. A signal lamp shows whether the heating is on or off.

1 Watertight connection made of silicone, in a modern heating cable, in 42 volt.
2 Totally enclosed stepdown transformer (250 watt 42 volt), for the safe operation of heating cable in the aquarium. A fuse protects the transformer against overload.

3.10.5.
Warmth from Below

As in nature, in a well functioning aquarium we must make sure that the water in the substrate is exchanged as slowly as possible. Undergravel filters and other systems have not proven their worth because water always follows the easiest path. Color tests have proven this convincingly.

Here we must use physical law, and warm the substrate from below. The rising warmth pushes old water up and automatically pulls new water from above into the substrate.

There is such a system of substrate heating. This heating system consists of a heating cable which has 42 volts of safety current. This heating cable is available in 8 versions. Six underwater heating cables for the substrate, and two additional heating cables for extra winter heating. These cables are all made of silicone, and because of their excellent flexibility can easily be installed on the aquarium bottom by means of cable anchors.

Gravel whichever the size, and other additional materials have no effect on this heating system, since this is not immersion heating, but warmth developing cables, separated from one another thus guaranteeing excellent thermal control. The heating cable will not be more than 2 degrees Celsius warmer than the surface temperature of the aquarium water, when the gravel size is 2 to 3 millimeters.

Since this system runs on 42 volts, it is completely safe even if the cable should be damaged at some point.

3.11.
Decoration

A natural biotope is naturally beautiful. In the case of an artificial biotope, man is taking a hand in the arrangement of his environment. For this reason we must try very hard not to exceed what is natural in our desire to arrange things. There are enough aquaristic decorative errors which show what a boundless desire to arrange, is capable of.

3.11.1.
In the Tropics

At one point during our observations in the jungle of South Thailand, we heard one of the participants in our expedition say to himself »this mud, contains so many organic substances, iron and more iron, if the Aquarists could only see this. If we could only bring a little of this into our aquarium, our aquarium would be terribly dirty.«

These spontaneous reflections were truly characteristic of our biotope observations. In speaking of decoration, we simply cannot depend on our observations

1 Cryptocoryne cordata (f. siamensis) in a morass in South Thailand.
2 Aponogeton rigidifolis in a murky stream in Sri Lanka.
3 Vallisneria americana, in fast flowing clear water, to our surprise in a stream in Ceylon. One can also observe plants in tropical waters which in fact have their origin elsewhere, but were somehow introduced. Through such spreading the fauna is mixed up.

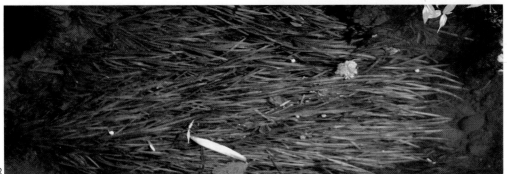

1

2

3

of nature. Our aquarium would then indeed be very dirty.

These observations are only important when we speak of nutrients and organic substances in aquarium water. They are not however, suitable as a basis for our aesthetic appreciation of the aquarium. We Aquarists want crystal clear water and beautiful healthy plant growth. If however, we are arranging our beautifully growing plants in a lovely underwater landscape, consisting of dead decorative materials such as stones and wood, this has nothing to do anymore with nature. It is also true that in the lovely cryptocoryne biotopes of South Thailand, we found, in certain places, only 5 types of water plants, of which at least 1, such as the *Crinum thaianum* with its 3.5 meter long leaves, could hardly be considered a standard type of plant for an aquarium.

In Choosing our plants we can take the entire world into consideration, whether it be South America, Thailand, India, China, Africa or whatever. No matter how lovely the decoration with dead material is, it is of course nonsensical, if the water plants themselves are not well chosen, or are placed clumsily in the aquarium. A good arrangement of water plants is also useless if they don't grow well, or if they suffer be cause of other environmental factors. These are the most important pre-requisites for the good decoration of an aquarium.

Underwater photography in a tropical stream. These photos clearly show that nature does not have a preference for a particular biotope when it comes to plants. Never will the diversity of plants in an aquarium be found in nature either. In nature the rule is a mono-culture: i. e. one, two, or maximum three species are to be found in any given area.
1 This is how a Cryptocoryne area in South Thailand in the vicinity of Lam Pi looks. C. cordata in between rests of non-aquatic plants, roots and fallen leaves, and wood.
2 Blyxa together with Cryptocorynes
3 Fallen leaves in a Cryptocoryne area. The depth by all photos averages 1,5 m to 2,0 m.

3.11.2.
In the Aquarium

The basic pre-requisite for good aquarium decoration is a decoration which is rich in types of water plants, and water plants which are able to grow well. There are of course those who do not agree with this type of Optimum Aquarium. They speak rather disdainfully of cheap vegetables. However, looking at the aquariums of these cheap vegetables aquarists, we usually find aquariums which scarcely enchant us. There are aquariums in which 3 or 4 years

1

ago, 3 or 4 different types of plants were planted, and in which since that time only 1 plant with a mono culture has flourished. In our Optimum Aquarium however, we are in a position to allow numerous tropical plants to flourish, and to use them as decoration and as a water conditioner.

Before we decorate our aquarium then, we should like to summarize the following:
- No natural sunlight,
- If possible, no see through aquariums,
- The aquarium should be wider than it is high,
- The aquarium should be correctly lighted.

If we now go to decoration with dead material, we should first of all think of the surface which we always see when we look in the aquarium, and that is the back wall. There are 2 possibilities to decorate the back wall:

The photos show pictures of successful underwater landscapes
1 Eichhornia azurea offers a focal view point
2 + 3 In these types of aquaria fish also feel at home.

- **Exterior** — there are variations which go from black paper to a picture of an aquarium. There is also the possibility of putting a wooden plate behind the aquarium which is decorated with cork and some land plants, in order to give an optical depth to the aquarium through the contours of the material. The decoration of the back wall of the aquarium from outside has one particular disadvantage and that is that the back wall glass may collect algae. This algae is problematic, because it is so difficult to reach and for this reason is rarely removed. To the back wall which has been so lovingly decorated from outside will disappear progressively behind the algae.
- **Interior** — it is also practical and this method has proven to be excellent, to simply put brown colored styrofoam plates with cork relief in the aquarium in front of the back wall. The styrofoam floats so it is necessary to clip it to back wall under the top pane. A back wall like this can also be provided with holes in which fern and java moss can be tied under water. This back wall can now become covered with algae without any problem, since with increasing age it becomes more and more a part of the aquarium decoration.

Lava stone is particularly suitable for back wall decoration, because the stones

3

can be positioned very nicely with silicone. In the gaps which then occur, such woods as Scottish Moore Oak, resinous pine wood and mangroves can be walled in. The silicone needs at least 3 hours until the next layer can be placed on top of the previous one. But if you wait 2 to 3 days you will have a beautiful and very long lived back wall.

Let us now consider the decoration of the water landscape itself. First of all, think about whether terraces are built rising towards the back or not. If they are built in this way, these terraces must be built very carefully since, because of the steady operation of the aquarium, and little »turm deckel« snails which get into the aquarium, anything unattached will be eveled, overtime. Here then the individual stones which are to be used to build a terrace must be bonded and attached with silicone.

After the tiers have been built, the intermediate areas can be filled to the desired height with aquarium gravel (don't forget the 42 volt heating cable and the laterite additive). Then another source of decoration such as resinous pine wood, Scottish moore oak, or bamboo stalks can be introduced. In the case of bamboo stalks we should like to mention that they rot in fresh water after 3 to 4 years.

The following materials are also at our disposal:

- Stones – basically any type of stone which passes the hydrochloric test negatively (to determine the presence of lime). In the hydrochloric test we put a drop of hydrochloric acid on a stone. If immediately upon contact foam appears on the stone, then this means that the stone contains lime and cannot be used in the aquarium. If the test is negative, there will be no foam and the stone is suitable for decoration.

- Stones such as basalt, slate, granite and lava are known to be lime free and excellently suited for decoration in our Optimum Aquarium. However, during decoration, one must keep in mind that the stones should not be thoughtlessly arranged. A lava stone, for example, does not look well next to slate, and a basalt doesn't look well next to granite. Furthermore, keep in mind that resinous pine wood look better with lava stone than with slate.

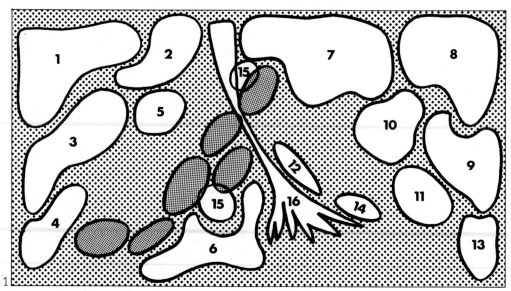

No.	Plant name and decoration	Number for size		
		130 cm	160 cm	200 cm
1	Vallisneria americana	20	30	50
2	Heteranthera zosterifolia	10	20	25
3	Hygrophila polysperma	20	40	60
4	Didiplis diandra	20	30	40
5	Eichhornia azurea	1	1	2
6	Echinodorus tenellus o. Lilaeopsis novae-zelandiae	50	100	150
7	Hygrophila difformis	10	15	20
8	Rotala rotundifolia	20	30	40
9	Hygrophila angustifolia	5	10	20
10	Limnophila aquatica	10	20	40
11	Rotala macrandra	10	20	30
12	Micranthemum umbrosum	10	20	40
13	Cryptocoryne parva	10	20	30
14	Aponogeton crispus	2	3	4
15	Microsorium pteropus	5	10	20
16	Moorkienwood	small	medium	large
▓	Lava rock			

Below are some tricks which make it easier to arrange the decorative elements.

● Resinous pine wood should be dipped in water frist, since it is otherwise very likely to float. However, it can also be held down with non-rusting steel screws in the aquarium. Suction caps, attached to the side pane can prevent the initial buoyancy of resinous pine wood

● Bamboo stalks can be placed in a synthetic plate containing holes, and then anchored directly on to the substrate under the gravel

● The types of stone which are suitable for the aquarium should be well washed, and allowed to dry before being placed in the aquarium and after being placed in the aquarium they should be tied with silicone firmly, but elasticly.

● When decorating the resinous pine wood e.g. with fern, one can cut grooves in the wood, in order to attach the fern firmly there.

● When putting wood into the aquarium, you should know that the water can become sour and tinted. It is recommended that you partially change the water after 14 days or 4 weeks and fertilize it.

● In the case of gravel, which certainly is also part of the decoration, it is worth mentioning that it too must be free of lime. Gravel size of 2 to 3 millimeters has proven very successful. A smaller size should only be used if you want to keep substrate fish such as catfish. Particularly the fine, armored, catfish *Corydoras* like to work at the substrate with their sensitive whiskers. If the substrate is sharp or rough, the whiskers will continuously be damaged. So parts of the aquarium can be later filled with fine gravel in places where it's been determined that the catfish particularly like to stay.

In looking at the following examples of decoration, please think of them as food for thought. Please do not force yourself to plan because you want to avoid having to correct something later in the aquarium which bothers you. For this planning will hardly ever be successful.

Finally we should like to mention that continuously cutting back, correcting and partial re-arranging of the water plants is part of the decoration, and retention of an

2

3

attractive aquarium. This is as important as the regular care of a flower box.

---

1 *The good mix between red and green, round and small leaf plants constitutes the range of this underwater landscape.*
2 *Cryptocorynes, as here C. becketii require the maximising of all requirements on a continuous basis.*

4.
Control

A car is only as good as the service it gets. Applied to the aquarium, this means that success is directly dependent on the control and care given by the Aquarist. Certainly there are many things in which one can afford to be negligent in the course of keeping an aquarium. However, there are at least as many developments in the aquarium which have to be corrected with great care. Our Optimum Aquarium has been filled in such a way that it's really quite easy to care for, with the exception of the cutting back of well growing plants.

We should like to present here a control and care checklist which will make it easier for you to proceed towards your goal. Then we will discuss each of the individual points in greater detail.

4.1. Health control of the fish. Please consider the clarity of the fins. A view from below to above makes this control easier.

4.2. Health control of the water plants. Here note any yellowing of the young stalks and brown holes, either round or jagged.

4.3. Algae control. Algae blooms in (see through) greasy algae, thread algae, brush algae.

4.4. Control of the filter and the pump. Filter mass change when there is a decrease in flow through.

4.5. Control of the CO_2 and pH.

4.6. Control of the iron content.

4.7. Control of the carbonate hardness (biogienic decalcification)

4.8. Control of the amount of food given by the feeder (Phosphate Test). If necessary, correct.

4.9. Control of the CO_2 bottles' content.

4.10. Control of the lamps. Lamp change.

4.11. Regular care without previous control.

4.11.1. Water change with plant fertilizer (copper test).

4.11.2. Adjustments to the CO_2 apparatus.

4.11.3. Cleansing of the glass panes.

4.11.4. Cleansing of the cover.

4.1.
Health Control of the Fish

Since we assume that you as an Aquarist observe your aquarium quite often, you will automatically notice whether your fish are

1

2

feeling well. There are different symptoms of malaise, (for example fast breathing, rubbing against the stones, restless behavior) which may have different causes. Changes in the skin and fins, such as the appearance of little pimples, dullness, the appearance of tumors, the appearance of fungi, deterioration, sore muzzles. All of these are sure signs that there is a health complication. If these symptoms do not occur and the fish still feel unwell, chemical changes in the water may be the reason.

Diseased fish.
1 Fish react to unfriendly water conditions with increased slime output
2 Bulgy eyes often are the result of deteriorated water quality
3 Underwater photo of a Pterophyllum altum in a large aquarium.

3

- Test the pH. PH values over 8 or under 6 may cause a malaise among the fish. If the pH value is over 8 check the supply of carbonic acid and correct if necessary. If the pH value is under 6 check whether too much carbonic acid is being provided and correct if necessary. In this case, you should also measure the carbonate hardness, since a carbonate hardness of 1 degree will cause a dip in acidity.
- Check the nitrite content and the oxygen. If nitrite is present, the reason is that there is insufficient nitrification in the aquarium. Nitrifying bacteria can be gotten through the following:
  - Seeding with old aquarium water in which there is no nitrite;
  - Addition of natural substrate to the old substrate;
- If the pH is correct and there is no nitrite, too little oxygen may cause the fish to breath too fast or to feel unwell. Please measure the oxygen content and compare the value with our oxygen saturation table.

A still better method of understanding the aquarium water is to measure oxygen consumption. Oxygen consumption is a measure of the organic load of the water. The oxygen consumption can be measured from the difference between the oxygen content of water directly after it has been taken, and that content after a consumption period of 48 hours. This is a measurement of the oxygen consumption by the micro-organisms in the water that decompose the organic compounds in 48 hours.

A measuring flask is needed to carry out this measurement. First, as described, the oxygen measuring should be carried out. Then fill the CO_2 measuring flask under water with aquarium water and close it tightly. This flask should then be stored in darkness for 48 hours. (If possible at a temperature under 20 degrees Celsius). Then from this bottle the measuring cylinder should be filled with water very carefully in order to measure, as described, the O_2 content. The difference between the 2 oxygen measurements is the oxygen consumption. For example, oxygen content upon taking the water: 7.5 milligrams per liter. Oxygen content after 48 hours 2.7 milligrams per liter, gives us oxygen consumption in (BSB_2) of 4.8 milligrams per liter.

If you note an oxygen deficit, or too high oxygen consumption, you must look for the reason for this disturbance.

The reasons for too little oxygen content in an aquarium are many: Too weak light, too little CO_2, lack of one or several nutrients, too many fish, a poorly cared for filter, too high an organic load, over feeding and so on.

On no account may the O_2 content in aquariums decrease to under 5.0 milligrams per liter. Some hardy types of fish (Carp, Labyrinth fish) can survive at lower values but most aquarium fish begin to suffer here. Furthermore, high oxygen deficits usually herald the end of the aquarium.

If there is an oxygen deficit, check the light interval, the CO_2 supply, and feeding, and correct where necessary.

When measuring the phosphate content, you can also, from the other side, get the nitrogen load of the water.

If there is too high a phosphate content, this means that the aquarium has too many fish or the amount of food being given is too high. One quick counter measure is always a water change. Don't forget to add plant fertilizer. Think, above all, of tracing the cause of your problems. If you find a high pH value which didn't bother your fish before, and the nitrite content is negative, and the oxygen is also correct, an ammonia toxification may be occurring. An immediate countermeasure here would be a water change and a reduction of the pH value by adding CO_2. If the pH value is under 7, ammonia changes into non-toxic ammonium which is an excellent plant fertilizer.

Every aquarist is pleased to have healthy fish in good shape
1 Apistogramma cacatuoides
2 Male Betta splendens, a bred variety
3 Male Papilichromis ramirezi

1

2

3

You will of course measure the temperature, but you should also check whether the heating unit stopped working temporarily or the water was over-heated. Please make sure that all the plugs are completely plugged in, and the dial on the electronic regulator is correctly set.

Rooms in which people smoke, should always be well ventilated, since, especially air breathing fish, such as Labyrinth fish, can react very sensitively to smoke.

Check also whether one of the members of your family has sprayed insect spray on the flowers, or in one of the corners of the room, because this can be poisonous to fish. So called air fresheners from spray cans, are also toxic for fish. In renovating a room, be careful that the paint and glue which you use for wall paper, carpets, or other items does not develop toxic fumes which can under certain circumstances easily kill the fish in the aquarium. If all of these tests are negative, concentrate on the fish and possible diseases.

It is not the intention of this book to consider all disease symptoms, since we would go completely beyond our boundaries if we were to do so. In this case, we should like to point out that there is special literature which describes all diseases in detail.

In this regard, we should like to point out one thing. If for any reason it is necessary to put medication into the aquarium, this usually has a stressful effect on the metabolism of the water plants. On the other hand, the good assimilation and the good growth of your plants will dissolve these medications much faster than an aquarium that does not use our system. So in the one case as in the other, you must give considerably higher dosages of the medication, for exmaple, against ichthyophthirius.

After caring for the animals, and we are presuming here that they in fact did become healthy, it is a good idea to filter the water which you prepared so carefully with high performance activated carbon for 24 hours, or, and this would naturally be considerably better, help the plants to intensive growth with a combination of water change of at least 30 %, and plant fertilizer.

One more important piece of advice. In many houses the water pipes are made of copper. Warm water boilers are often provided with copper heating spirals. With the result that the tap water that flows into the aquarium has a high copper concentration. Under certain circumstances, this can kill the fish, but it will always disturb the balanced supply of nutrients which we consider so important. For this reason test your tap water for copper before it goes into the aquarium. The copper can easily be removed from the tap water, by letting the water run a while before filling the aquarium. A copper test will prove this.

4.2.
Health Control of Aquarium Plants

If your water plants become yellow, or round brown holes appear on the leaves, there is usually a lack of nutrients. This lack of nutrients can naturally have various causes. First of all check whether the carbon dioxide, light, plant fertilizer, substrate additive and water movement are all optimal. The iron test is particularly useful in determining whether the nutrients supply is optimal.

If everything is in order here, you should not see these symptoms in your water plants.

Often mistakes are made, for example in water changes, no plant fertilizer is given, because it's forgotten, or you neglected to turn on the switch timer, or some dear family member turned off the aquarium lighting for economic reasons. Check each of these things. If your are a particularly forgetful person and can't continuously supply liquid fertilizer, use a nutrient pump which takes over this function automatically.

We should also like to point out here that the water which is added because of evaporation of the aquarium water, should not be provided with nutrients since during the evaporation process the nutrients remain in the aquarium and in fact become even more concentrated.

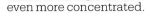

1 Hygrophila corymbosa is a prized plant as it consumes a lot of nitrate in the aquarium. It grows fast and has to be trimmed back often.

1

If you do see round or jagged holes on the leaves of your water plants, some snails can be the reason, since they do cause this type of damage. If you find this to be the case, you can crush the snails and feed them at regular intervals to the fish, or you can put a puffer fish in the aquarium for a short time, which will quickly take care of the snail problem. (Figure 8 puffer)

Another aspect of plant health control, is careful observation and regulation of their growth. It is all too natural that plants grow towards the light and thus preffer to expand directly beneath the water surface. The shade which is caused by this, causes in turn a lack of light for the plants underneath and the entire system of the aquarium can be disturbed. Therefore the plants must be cut back to an acceptable length.

There is a trick in the case of the Amazone sword plants. If you always cut back the newest leaves you force the plant to grow a smaller leaf the next time. In this way this plant can be kept to a controlled size. Vallisneria can simply be cut with a pair of scissors to the height of the water level without damaging the plant. You have to be careful that Sagittaria and warf amazone plants do not choke each other. For this reason they should always be kept apart and rearranged.

The floating plants on the watersurface, should not be allowed to reproduce too much, since they too can cause an undesired light reduction.

1 Cryptocoryne balansae rarely is subject to the famous Cryptocoryne diseases in an aquarium
2 Alternanthera with staggered effect.

4.3.
Algae Control

The important and indispensable control of algae consists of discovering the conditions under which an algae plague can occur in time. Warning signals in the aquarium of a possible algae danger are, too high nitrate and above all else high phosphate values. With the modern analysis procedures, which are at the disposal of the modern Aquarist it is entirely possible, even for those Aquarists who do not know chemistry, to carry out this control procedure. Phosphate values of more than 1.0 milligrams per liter when occurring together with a high amount of nitrate mean algae danger. A counter measure, which is to be recommended, as in the case of nitrate, is frequent water changes, and the use of fast growing plants.

If you look through the length of the aquarium you will be able to see the development of an algae bloom relatively early, particularly during the spring. It appears green and cloudy when you look through it. Normally it has been recommended that a water change be carried out, but in the case of an algae bloom this is entirely erroneous. Chemical preparations are also too radical and will harm the plant growth.

In this case only an ultra violet steriliser can help and will take care of the algae bloom within a week. However, the ultraviolet steriliser harms the complicated nutrient complex of aquarium fertilizer. For this reason, after the water has become clear, change it partially and then add fertilizer. The algae bloom can also be removed by means of a diatomeous or silica algae filter. These are special filters which have a filter substrate out of diatomeous earth, finer than the floating algae themselves. In this way the water can be filtered crystal clear relatively quickly.

If you discover smear algae, which is known as blue algae, this indicates a temporary instability in the aquarium. Smear algae which can develop very fast in favorable conditions, can be caused in the initial period after the aquarium has been set up, by the plant lamps such as gro-lux and fluora. If, after changing the lamps, and

using biological warfare, you can't get rid of the smear algae, you don't have any choice but to fight the algae with algicide. After 4 to 5 days the amount of algicide will have reduced itself without having disturbed the entire system too much. During this time you must not filter with carbon or artificial resin. But you may retain your mechanical filtration. Remember that blue or smear algae must be taken seriously. They grow very fast and can win the race in the end, if they grow over all the plants within days.

In the case of thread and brush algae, we are dealing with higher algae which can be stunted in their growth during their development without a biological algae preventative. If however thread algae do occur you'll be consoled to know that they can be removed easily from plants with mechanical devices or with other decoration material. The so called brush or beard algae, will only be found on damaged water plant leaves or on dead decoration material. The occurrence of thread algae is usually a sign of good water conditions, because they can only grow in aquariums which are functioning well. An increase in this type of algae can best be prevented with fish, particu-

1 The Java fern, Microsorium pteropus can be attached in the aquarium with Nylon thread or wood, roots or other decoration.

larly with the Veil Tail Molly. This is also true for brush algae. The antennae catfish mentioned in chapter 3.8.1. eat and continually scrape off the new shoots of brush algae.

If all your attemps fail you can support the work of the fish by adding algicide to the aquarium water, in order to stunt the algae growth. Unfortunately, thread algae cannot be entirely removed with any algicide without simultaneously damaging other water plants.

4.4.
Pump and Filter Control

Check at regular intervals whether your filter continues to work at peak performance. If this is not the case, the filter, and/or the prefilter, should be cleaned. Remember however, to leave a small amount of filter mass in the filter so that the nitrification bacteria remain. As in any abundantly growing garden, leaves fall also in our Optimum Aquarium. These plant remains usually gather in front of the suction basket of the impeller pump and the filter. This can considerably decrease their performance. For this reason remember ro remove plant remains from the filter and suction baskets, at regular intervals.

4.5.
Control of CO_2 and pH

Since the pH and CO_2 are dependent on one another, we should also like to consider them together. In the appendix you will see a newly edited CO_2 table from which you can easily tell which pH or CO_2 value you should have in order to retain a neutral pH at a given carbonate hardness. For example, with a carbonate hardness of 5 degrees you need 23 milligrams of free carbon dioxide in order to reach a pH of 6.8.

You can easily read this balance by means of a small measuring device which shows the colors blue, green or yellow. Yellow is the acidic area which means that there is too much CO_2. Green is the neutral area which is desired. The pH here is between 6 and 7.2. Blue indicates an alkaloid area which means there is too little CO_2.

Since we want to have a neutral pH in our Optimum Aquarium, and indeed must have one, since this is also important for the CO_2 assimilation of water plants, we must regulate the CO_2 supply in order to achieve the desired value.

This practical measurement is however only qualitative. The quantitative measurement of course gives us more exact values. When undertaking to measure the CO_2 we should have 100 or 200 milliliters of test water in order to have a maximum error of 1 milligram per liter.

If we don't keep a neutral pH, or CO_2 saturation, the plants are forced to start bicarbonate assimilation (to take carbon out of the bicarbonates) and this will decrease the carbonate hardness. With the carbonate hardness under 1 degree there is the danger of an acid drop, which means that the pH drops very fast into an area which is deadly for fish. We can avoid and balance out bicarbonate assimilation as follows:

1. We must make sure that there is sufficient CO_2 in the aquarium and,
2. We should change the water more often in order to increase the carbonate hardness.

The CO_2 or pH test however, is only accurate if with each water change you put new water and reagent into the indicator.

The carbonate hardness test will show you whether bicarbonate assimilation is taking place, if you compare the water with which you fill the aquarium with the water in the aquarium. If you see different values here, i.e. if the carbonate hardness of the aquarium water is lower than the fresh water, bicarbonate assimilation or biogienic decalcification is occurring. In this case you have not provided the aquarium with sufficient carbon dioxide. You should correct the amount of CO_2 immediately.

4.6.
Control of Carbonate Hardness

You should measure the carbonate hardness when you fill the aquarium with new tap water. In the case of later measurement, for example after 2 to 3 weeks, a difference in the new water can only mean that biogienic decalcification has occurred. In this case there is not enough CO_2, a condition which should be corrected as soon as possible. (see Chapter 4.5.). When measuring the carbonate hardness we should like to point out that in many cities the water hardness can fluctuate because of the mixing of soft and hard water. For this reason you should always note down the values you found upon first measuring so that you have something with which to compare later results (analytic journal).

4.7.
Food Control

The amount given to our fish should be balanced. If we delegate the feeding of the fish to a family member, we should also control the amount of food being given, from time to time.

Over-feeding leads to food remains, which can have a negative effect on the quality of the water. Furthermore if the fish do not get enough to eat, their stomachs fall, and they become sick and usually cannot be saved.

If you measure the phosphate or nitrate content at intervals of 14 days, you'll be able to see whether the load on the aquarium is rising or dropping, because of corrective measures.

4.8.
Nutrient Control

We have learned from the preceeding chapter about the continual supply which natural waters obtain of the most important plant nutrients, particularly of the critical ones, by means of nutrient springs. In the aquarium too we use daily liquid preparations that contain the critical nutrients in order to achieve this continuity. The control of these critical nutrients is best done with an iron test. An iron content of .1 milligrams per liter is desirable, as we have described in detail in Chapter 3.4.6.

Since the supply of these critical nutrients in the aquarium is dependent on a number of factors such as plant mass, food, light, warmth and so on, weekly controls are absolutely necessary. Often you'll discover that at times, too much or too little fertilizer had been given. You will also observe that a newly set up aquarium, in its initial phase, needs larger amounts of fertilizer, than in the later phase. Possibly depot and ion exchange processes play a role here. Timely correction secures nutrient supply in any case.

If you use a nutrient pump for liquid fertilizing with Dupla Plant 24, you must measure the iron content every day during the initial period in order to set the amount of liquid fertilizer that comes out of the nutrient pump exactly according to need.

At this point we should like to point out that it is very important to write down the values you find on the day of the measurement, giving the date and the time since we can only make corrections by comparing. The modern Aquarist uses an analytic journal which is available on the market.

4.9.
Carbon Control

Carbon control is very important since we must make sure that this important nutrient is continually supplied to the aquarium plants. For this control it is necessary, when the bottle pressure in the CO_2 depot (gas bottle) decreases, to change it within the next 48 hours (Replacement bottle).

4.10.
Lighting Control

It's always good to note on your calendar the day on which you put up new flourescent tubes, or mercury vapor lamp over your aquarium. Then you can set a date on which you want to measure the light. When you first set up the light, start with a general light measurement (any light meter will do) and then measure the light after a certain time, for example 6 months. You can see from the difference in light value at what point you have to change your lamp.

4.11.
Regular Care Activity without Previous Control

Along with the measures that we've described up until now, there are of course other things to be taken care of, which while they have no control function, are of great importance for the smooth functioning of our aquarium.

4.11.1.
Water Change with Aquarium Fertilizer

We already mentioned in earlier chapters that an Optimum Aquarium should have a water change of 30 to 50 % every month. This is particularly important in the initial phase of the aquarium. We achieve two very important things with water changes;

● Nutrient peaks such as Nitrogen in the form of nitrate and humin materials from resinous pine wood and fish, are eliminated.

● Nutrient lows which occur in the case of iron, manganese and other important nutrients, can be eliminated by water changes and aquarium fertilizer. Always add the correct amount of aquarium fertilizer, in accordance with the amount of water changed.

Traditionally the water change occurred by means of a suction hose and a bucket which was placed in front of the aquarium. This was always an irritant for the house-

1 The aquarium is placed in a ledge between two pillars, light: 3 fluorescent tubes, 3 × 30 watt

wife, because water change rarely occurs without some water being splashed around. Since in the case of the Optimum Aquarium we are certainly not talking about smal aquariums, a water amount of at least 60 to 100 liters will have to be transported. For this you should use, instead of a bucket, a long garden hose, which you can place in the bathroom for a short period of time. Put two suction devices and a filter strainer on the end of the hose which you are going to put into the aquarium, in order to safely install this end of the hose in the aquarium. Suck hard on the other end and you'll see how simple the water change can be.

While the water is being changed, you can clean the panes from within, cut the plants back, and clean the filter strainer of the submerged impeller driven pump and of the filter. Then you only need to wait until the water change mark has been reached. This mark is a signal which is put on the outside of the aquarium, and which shows exactly to what depth your water level in the aquarium must sink in order to change 30 to 50 % of the water. You can calculate the water amounts later by using a ruler to measure your aquarium according to the formula $A \times B \times C =$ length $\times$ breadth $\times$ height.

When filling the aquarium, you only need to connect the end of the hose out of which the water is running with a hose attachement to the fittings in the bathroom, in order to fill the aquarium again with temperate water.

A tip: Try not to splash any water around when you are re-winding the hose since some water will still be in it.

Remember also, as we mentioned above, that if you have copper pipes in the house, the first water out of the tap can contain copper. Let the water run for about 15 minutes and you will have copper free water (Cu test).

4.11.2.
Providing Carbon Dioxide

The care of the CO_2 apparatus is very important, like the water change with plant fertilizer.

Control the number of bubbles in the contact pipe of the CO_2 Reactor 400 (Dupla) or if you have a complete system, read the pH value on the pH continuous regulator. If the pH value is too low, or too high, you can set the desired pH value by means of a dial for if necessary re-calibrate the pH electrode.

4.11.3.
Cleaning the Panes

We hope that you consider everything that we have recommended as reasonable and sensible. We also assume that you are also interested in regularly cleaning the outside and the inside panes of your aquarium. Then you will have pleasure with your aquarium. There are a number of very good cleaning instruments on the market today.

4.11.4.
Cleaning the Cover

The cover should be cleaned at every water change. Since covers which have been soiled with algae and by water hardness, can filter the light considerably, and reduce the intensity of the lighting by a large number of lux.

Note: There are cleaning products for glass wich are poisonous for fish. Remember to always clean the glass panes with clear water. You can easily remove lime around the edges, with a drop of hydrochloric acid, but you must rinse carefully.

5.
A Word at the End

This book, dear reader, has been written by practitioners, by Aquarists who have been studying aquaristics for decades, and who are questioning some old traditions and for-mulating new knowledge into modern aquaristic rules. All the conclusions that we drew from our observations in the native waters of the aquarium fish and plants, and from enumerable experiments, were tested first intensively in our own aquariums.

The Optimum Aquarium which we have presented to you is a type of aquarium in which most aquarium fish and plants can

1

live, and be cared for together without any problem, and independent of the chemical and physical make-up of the tap or well water being used. Furthermore, in this type of aquarium, fish and plants are partners in an artificial, but fully functional biotope. An artificial biotope which has its own laws. It was from the very beginning our aim to remove the aquarium from the realm of the happy coincidence or the green thumb. We owe it to the animals and plants with which we are entrusted. To give them a calculated and programmed environment and not a medium which is adventurous and full of risks.

The great experience which we have collected over the last decades, with this type of aquarium, assures us that you will have much pleasure and success with your aquarium, provided you follow the rules set forth in this book.

We have heard of enumerable success from the numbers of letters, telephone calls, and personal conversations we have had, and many frustrated Aquarists who would have given up the hobby, have confirmed their success to us with great enthusiasm.

If from time to time an Aquarist was unhappy with his aquarium (»although I followed your suggestions point for point«) an exact analysis of his aquarium always showed that some error had been committed somewhere. The response was always, »Oh I thought that would'nt be so important«.

In many cases, the Aquarist gets experience with the law of nature, which is known in botany, as the »Liebig Minimum Law«. In aquaristic terms this means that good growth of plants is greatly influenced by the smallest growth factor. According to this for example, an increased use of plant fertilizer is of no use if at the same time there is too little CO_2 or energy (= too little light).

In this regard we should like to point once again to the ten points for success in the Optimum Aquarium which we presented at the beginning of the practical part of this book.

5.1.
The Tested Example

In this book you have seen pictures of aquariums which we have kept and cared for over the years, and in which we have repeatedly tested our ideas concerning the Perfect or Optimum Aquarium. Now we would like to talk in somewhat more detail about an aquarium about which you may have read someplace else and which you may even have seen at one point. We are talking about the large 10 000 liter aquarium which Horst E. Kipper set up in his house twenty years ago. Since then thousands of Aquarists have stood before this aquarium, photographed it, measured it and taken home ideas for their own aquarium. This aquarium, which was originally set up as a sea water aquarium has provided a testing ground for the avant garde ideas of the authors since 1972. But before we speak of the set-up, and experience with this large aquarium, here are some facts concerning its history.

5.1.1.
The History

When Horst E. Kipper planned his house in 1966/67 the aquarium already existed on paper. It was to be placed in the lower level in its own room, with a filter chamber, and corresponding laboratory. Some people made fun of the fact that it seemed that the house was being built for the aquarium, which was good for the optimization of the aquarium.

At first Horst E. Kipper set up a sea water aquarium with a coral reef with numerous coral fish according to natural models. Aquarists and experts were amazed with the water circulation device, the fully automatic filter and the water cleaning apparatus. Reports on these aspects appeared in many domestic and foreign professional journals. In the meantime, the ideas of a new and modern fresh water hobby had grown to the point, that they were already being tested in many aquariums, and being continually im-

1
1969

2
1972

proved upon, and changed. It was decided to change the 10 000 liter aquarium, and to use it as a testing ground for the new aquaristic concepts. Furthermore, the existing sea water aquarium was exhibiting some problems, which because of its unusual size were at that time difficult to solve.

In 1972 the aquarium was rebuilt into a fresh water aquarium. All the factors which were known as pre-requisites for a well functiong aquarium were taken into consideration. Professor Dr. Joachim Schulze of Berlin who saw the aquarium soon thereafter wrote in the journal »The Aquarium« (5/74),» I was convinced when I saw this viewing tank with its overwhelming beautiful plant growth, that an optimization of all growth conditions can lead to wonderful results. I am sure that similarly favorable growing conditions can be realized in more modestly sized aquariums and with simpler technical apparatus.«

We agreed with Schulze's last sentence and we described this in our book, The Perfect Aquarium, in detail.

This aquarium was a joy to be seen for 10 years before it started to show signs of fatigue. In spite of all attempts to stimulate plant growth with more light, fertilization and CO_2 the total picture was becoming increasingly unsatisfactory.

These experiences and the reason for them finally led to changes in some major points which we had recommended for a perfect aquarium. The new set up of this aquarium took place in 1983/84 and thus began the era of the Optimum Aquarium.

1 The Dupla large aquarium (2500 gallons) in its marine version from 1969 to 1972
2 Shortly after its change-over to freshwater in 1972. Already then Mercury vapor lamps were installed, which started a revolution in aquarium lighting methods.

5.1.2.

The Proving Ground – The 10 000 Liter Aquarium

Many Aquarists may be surprised that we consider the use of our rules for an Optimum Aquarium in a 10 000 liter large aquarium, to be a particular testing ground. At first glance one would think that greater volume secures greater stability. This is however, not the case in practice as the following considerations make clear. The higher an aquarium is, the worse the ratio of water surface to content. This is usually not sufficiently appreciated because of the gas exchange with the atmosphere. For example, an aquarium measuring $50 \times 50 \times 150$ centimeters = (height $\times$ depth $\times$ width) = 375 liters, has a surface factor of 20 (20 centimeters squared per liter). An aquarium that is only 40 centimeters high with the same depth and width has a factor of 25.

The large aquarium with the measurements of 610 centimeters long, 200 centimeters deep and 80 centimeters water level (absolute height 110 centimeters) has a surface factor of only 12.5 i.e. 12.5 centimeters squared per liter.

Enormous amounts of movement energy are necessary in order to mix all the nutrients regularly, and to achieve the same temperatures in all areas. Large amounts of light and energy are necessary in order to provide enough light in the substrate zone, for the plants which are growing there, which are mostly hungry for light. Furthermore, water changes of at least 1/3 of the contents every 14 days, means that in this period of time 3250 liters of water must be changed which translates into a daily portion of 230 liters.

One factor which is hardly a problem in a medium sized aquarium, is for example the removal of sick or dead fish, of rotting plant parts, of decayed substances and occasionally of individual strands of algae or parts of algae, all of which quickly becomes very problematic in a large aquarium. In other words, in a very large aquarium, there are many things that have to regulate themselves, which in a smaller aquarium can be

regulated with the help of the Aquarist. At no time however, may a large growth of algae or a water bloom occur in a large aquarium. A blue algae plague in a 100 liter aquarium can easily be overcome in a short period of time. At the worst you are risking having to set up the aquarium again. However, in a 10 000 liter aquarium with more than a thousand fish and thousands of plants, an algae plague would simply be a catastrophe. And furthermore can you imagine how the entire hous would smell if a blue algae plague occurred on this scale?

1 After 11 years as a freshwater aquarium the 2 500 gallon Dupla Aquarium was rebuilt once more. Horst E. Kipper during the transformation
2 The empty aquarium. Even the old bottom was thrown away, as it proved to be the growth limiting factor, after 11 years. New quartz gravel, 2–3 mm, was put in, mixed with an iron containing compound.

5.1.3.
Set up and Operation

Here are, first of all the technical details concerning the large aquarium system:

5.1.3.1.
Lighting

Lighting is taken care of by ten 250 watt Metal Halide Lamps, which are hung 100 centimeters above the water surface. Furthermore two 90 x 120 centimeter dormer windows were built into the ceiling. The lighting values in the aquarium measured on a day in October were as follows: Directly under the laps: 20 000 lux on the water surface, falling to 4000 lux at 70 centimeters depth. Next to a lamp 5000 lux were measured on the water surface falling to 750 lux at 70 centimeters depth. On the leaf surface of the plants lux values between 800 and 2 500 were measured.

The lighting time was between 8 (4 lamps) and 10 hours (6 lamps).

5.1.3.2.
The Substrate

The substrate consists of 2 to 3 millimeters strong quartz gravel, which was mixed in the lower layer with 25 liters of Duplarit (tropical Laterite) with a high iron content. The height of this layer was 10 to 23 centimeters. In total 1.2 tons of quartz gravel and substrate additive were mixed. The back walls and buildings were formed from lava rock with cement with a low lime content.

In contrast to the old set up, in which only 4 millimeter quartz gravel was used, the quartz gravel used here had 2 to 3 millimeters diameter. One of the possible reasons for the natural end of the first fresh water period, of the aquarium after 11 years, was that the substrate had become too dense over the course of time, and had developed a substrate layer which could no longer be penetrated by the plant roots. Decayed material (food and plant remnants)

1 The large Dupla aquarium shortly after its transformation
2 A few weeks later all plants had grown and some were reaching the surface already
3 The aquarium after approxemately 6 months. In the foreground, a thick carpet of Lilaeopsis-nova-zelandiae had grown. Also Anubias barteri var., nana had multiplied considerably. The aquarium was again a pleasure to the eye.

settled between the rougher gravel and was mineralized by bacteria. Finally this had the same effect as natural cement, and baked the substrate layer together as if it were concrete. When gravel, with a smaller diameter (2 to 3 millimeters) which we now recommend for all aquariums, was used, the decayed matter remained above the gravel, and thus was more easily transported into the prefilter and into the filter.

5.1.3.3.
Heating

Before the substrate was set up 54 meters of heating cable out of silicone, with a strength of 340 watts/42 volts was placed on the bottom of the aquarium. The water temperature in the aquarium is held at exactly 25 degrees Celcius by means of an electronic regulator (Duplatherm).

5.1.3.4.
Filtration

A modern trickle dry filter system takes care of the filtration, and it consists of a pre-filter and cotton, a main filter with Dupla-bioballs, as a filter body, and a fine or mesh filter made of layers of synthetic material. This trickle filter can turn over 4000 liters per hour. In addition, 4 impeller driven pumps with individual strength of 4200 liters each, see to it that the aquarium is completely turned over 1 1/2 times an hour.

5.1.3.5.
Water Change and Fertilization

A timing device takes care of changing 260 liters of water a day. A dosing pump automatically adds corresponding amounts of plant fertilizer (Duplaplant) as a basic fertilizer and Duplaplant 24 as a daily fertilizer, as well as the corresponding amount of a water preparation called Duplagan.

The Dupla pH Continuous Controller automatically regulates the amount of CO_2 provided, and the pH value is set at 7. The Dupla-CO_2-Reactor-S is used for CO_2 diffusion.

5.1.3.6.
Water Values

Temperature: 25° Celcius
Total Hardness: 12° dH
Carbonate Hardneass: 10° dH
pH Value: 7.0
CO_2: 28 milligrams to a liter
Iron (FE 2 + 3): 0.08 milligrams per liter
Copper: 0 milligrams per liter
Nitrite: 0 milligrams per liter
Nitrate: 25 milligrams per liter
Phosphate: Trace
Conductivity: 550 microsiemens
Oxygen: Fluctuates between 88 to 90 % in the morning and 110 to 112 % in the evening. This corresponds to an absolute O_2 content of 7 to 10 milligrams per liter.

5.1.3.7.
The Plant List

The more than 50 different types of tropical marsh and water plants give an aesthetically beautiful, and total impression, and above all else guarantee sufficient oxygen for the fish and the bacteria. The oxygen content fluctuates between 88 to 90 % in the morning when the light source is turned on and 110 to 112 % when the light diminishes. In absolute values this means there is a fluctuation from 7 to 9 milligrams per liter of O_2. Of course, over time during the year some types of plants are exchanged. However, the amount of the regularly lighted plants is a proof of how productively the optimal system works.

At the time of writing there were the following types of plants in the aquarium:
Alternanthera reineckii, Ammannia senegalensis, Anubias afzeli, A. barteri var. *barteri, A. barteri* var. *nana; Aponogeton boivianus, Bacopa amplexicaulis, Bolbitis heudelotii, Cabomba caroliniana, Crinum thaianum, Cryptocoryne albida, C. affinis,*

C. balansae, C. moehlmannii, C. parva, C. pontederiifolia, C. wendtii, C. willisii, Didiplis diandra, Echinodorus argentinensis, E. bleheri, E. cordifolus spec. mini, E. grisebachii, E. horemanii, E. horizontalis, E. maior, E. osiris, E. parviflorus, E. tenellus parvulus, Egeria densa, Heteranthera zosterifolia, Hydrocotyle leucocephalus, Hygrophila corymbosa, H. difformis, Lilaeopsis novae-zelandiae, Lobelia cardinalis, Ludwigia palustris x repens, Marsilia crenata, Mayaca vandellii, Micranthemum umbrosum, Microsorium pteropus, Nesea crassicaulis, Nuphar japonica, Nymhaea lotus Rot, Nymphoides humboldtiana, Riccia fluitans, Rotala macrandra, R. rotundifolia, R. wallichii, Vallisneria asiatica, V. gigantea, Vesicularia dubyana.

5.1.3.8.
The Fish List

When the aquarium was set up again in the spring of 1984, a total of 700 fish of 20 different types were placed in the aquarium. Naturally there are many more since then, and they cannot be counted. Some types have reproduced to such an extent that special methods of catching them will have to be worked out soon, (for example with wire baskets) because they can no longer be caught with the traditional means. The fish list as per the last set up follows.

In front of this aquarium, since its inception many years ago, uncountable discussions with Hobbyists and scientific people have taken place. Many ideas which have been applied in the hobby took root here.
1 Nuphar pumila grows very elegantly here in mounds and valleys
2 Nymphaea lotus (Red Lotus) over and over again entices the photographer to catch the beauty of its inflorescence.
3 Hygrophila corymbosa can, because of the 80 cm height grow to its true beauty
4 (next page) Melanotaenia boesemani, the Australian rainbowfish
5 The Dupla 2500 gallon aquarium seen through a photographer's fish-eye lens.

Ancistrus leucos (20), *Astynax* spec. (50), *Aphyocharax rathbuni* (50), *Cheirodon axelrodi* (120), *Corydoras arcuata* (5), *C. barbatus* (10), *Epalzeorhynchus siamensis* (10), *Farlowella acus* (20), *Hemiodus gracilis* (20), *Hyphessobrycon erythrostigma* (50), *Lamprologus brichardi* (10), *Melanotaenia boesemani* (100), *Petitella georgiae* (65), *Poecilia latipinna* (50), *Rasbora heteromorpha* (20), *Steatocranus casuarius* (10), *Synodontis nigriventus* (20), *Tetraodon steindachneri* (2), *Triportheus* spec. (50), *Pterygophichthys anisitsi* (18).

Possibly, some Aquarists will not agree with our mix of types. They will find fish which generally do not get on well with one another. Some come from acidic natural waters, others swim in their native environment in alkaline waters. We wanted this in our aquarium though, because we wanted to demonstrate that the golden mean can be achieved with a neutral pH, which allows the large spectrum of fish and water plants to enjoy a common and optimal environment.

Standing before the aquarium, a beautiful school swims by. *Melanotaenia boesemani,* the Australian Rainbow Fish. This beautiful school of healthy superb fish represents a living bond to the new home of my co-author and friend, Horst E. Kipper, who now lives in Australia.

4

5

6. APPENDIX

6.1. Checklist for the balanced and successful care of the Optimum Aquarium

Control:

1
Health control of the fish:
Please note that the fins should be clear; view from top to bottom facilitates control.

2
Health control of the water plants:
Check for yellowing of young shoots, brown and round holes, jagged holes; Fe-test.

3
Algae control:
Algae bloom (see-through), smear algae, thread algae, brush algae: PO_4-Test.

4
Control of the outflow of filter water: change filter mass if flow is sharply reduced.

5
Control of the straining device of the underwater impeller driven pump, and of the filter.

6
Control of the CO_2 level: CO_2-test

7
Control of the carbonate hardness (SBK) (biogenic decalcification)/ KH-test.

8
Control of plants and floating plants on the water surface.

9
Control of the amount of food given by the feeder: if necessary, correct.

10
Filling control of the CO_2 bottle.

11
Control of the lamps:
Change the fluorescent tubes. Regular care not requiring previous control.

12
Water change, with Duplaplant.

13
Cleaning of the panes, inside and outside.

14
Cleaning of the cover pane.

6.2. Plan for the establishment of an aquarium, e.g. for 130 × 60 × 45 cm = 350 Liter (approx. 90 gallons)

We recommend that you establish the aquarium as per the list below, then install the instruments, decorate, plant, and add the fish.

1. Establishment based on your shopping list.

1. Check the place where the aquarium is to be set up for light, temperature (constant-fluctuating), electrical outlets, security of the electrical apparatus, 220 volts in Europe and other countries, 115 volts in the United States.

2. Check the state of the floor (parquet, plaster, carpet).

3. Set up the lower portion of the aquarium and make sure that it is horizontal using a level.

4. Install a five-part electrical outlet and connect it to the electrical wiring.

5. Use hard styrofoam, cut to fit an aquarium of 130 x 60 cm, as a bottom layer under your aquarium and as protection against shock.

6. Clean the inside and the outside of the aquarium. If you install a 42 volt cable heater, it should be mounted so, that it is evenly spread over the glass bottom of the aquarium.

7. The electronic controls should be attached to the outlet, and the feeler secured with a vacuum cap to the aquarium.

8. Install the back-decoration wall of the aquarium.

9. Wash 70 liters of gravel. Clean all decorative elements such as resin pine wood, stones, etc., well.

10. Fill the filter with filter material.

11. Install hoses and other cables.

12. Install the underwater impeller-driven pump. Note: Place the vacuum basket at least 5 cm above the substrate bottom.

13. Connect the lighting to the feeding device or the timing device, set the desired times for turning on and off, e.g. from 10 a.m. to 10 p.m., but never more than 10–12 hours; check that it is working.

14. Substrate additive (Duplarit): mix about 1000 g with about 20 liters gravel.

15. Evenly distribute the mixture in the dry aquarium.

16. Put about 50 liters of the washed gravel without water in the aquarium.

17. Place the cleaned decorative material in the aquarium, and decorate (build terraces, eye-catchers at the back). Think about the plants when you are doing this.

18. *Slowly* fill the aquarium with tepid water (use clamps to attach the water change hose in the bathroom). Don't let the water flow in, on only one side, but distribute it over the entire substrate area.

19. Fill the aquarium up to the halfway point.

2. Installation

20. Plant according to example. Remove bad leaves beforehand, and also cut the roots by a third.

21. Fill up with water and don't forget to add fertilizer and water additives (Duplagan).

22. Install the CO_2 instrument and turn it on according to the instructions. It's a good idea to check the carbonate hardness at this point.

23. Install the check-valve in the CO_2 connection.

24. Install the CO_2-test, filled with indicator, and with aquarium water, making sure it is visible for CO_2 flow control.

25. Install the thermometer so that it is visible.

26. Set the thermostat at 25–26 degrees Celcius (76–78° F).

27. Turn on the filter and the underwater impeller-driven pump.

28. Remove plant remains.

29. Carefully clean the glass panes from the inside.

30. Put on the cover panes.

31. Turn on the lighting.

32. Control the function of the timer, e.g. 10 p.m.

33. Check the functioning of all electrical devices.

34. Note the date of installation, and the water and light levels on this day, which you have determined by tests. This is important for the fluorescent tube change after 12 months, among other tings. Use an analytic journal for this.

3. Installation

35. Put in algae-eating fish (10 *Epalzeorhynchus siamensis*, 6 *Peocilia sphenops*, 2 *Ancistrus dolichopterus*). Do not feed these fish for 14 days, which will force them to eat algae.

4. Installation

36. After two weeks, put in the rest of the fish and carefully begin to feed them.

5. Installation – after three month

37. Remove some plants and replace them with more sensitive water plants. Put in some more sensitive fish of your choice. Be careful not to have more than 1 cm fish per 2 liters aquarium water.

6.3. CO$_2$-Table

	Optimum CO$_2$ levels										
	Too much CO$_2$		optimum Level		Too little CO$_2$						
KH \ pH	6.0	6.2	6.4	6.6	6.8	7.0	7.2	7.4	7.6	7.8	8.0
0.5	15	9.3	5.9	3.7	2.4	1.5	0.93	0.59	0.37	0.24	0.15
1.0	30	18.6	11.8	7.4	4.7	3.0	1.86	1.18	0.74	0.47	0.30
1.5	44	28	17.6	11.1	7.0	4.4	2.8	1.76	1.11	0.70	0.44
2.0	59	37	24	14.8	9.4	5.9	3.7	2.4	1.48	0.94	0.59
2.5	73	46	30	18.5	11.8	7.3	4.6	3.0	1.85	1.18	0.73
3.0	87	56	35	22	14	8.7	5.6	3.5	2.2	1.4	0.87
3.5	103	65	41	26	16.4	10.3	6.5	4.1	2.6	1.64	1.03
4.0	118	75	47	30	18.7	11.8	7.5	4.7	3.0	1.87	1.18
5.0	147	93	59	37	23	14.7	9.3	5.9	3.7	2.3	1.47
6.0	177	112	71	45	28	17.7	11.2	7.1	4.5	2.8	1.77
8.0	240	149	94	59	37	24	14.9	9.4	5.9	3.7	2.4
10	300	186	118	74	47	30	18.6	11.8	7.4	4.7	3.0
15	440	280	176	111	70	44	28	17.6	11.1	7.0	4.4
20	590	370	240	148	94	59	37	24	14.8	9.4	5.9

CO$_2$ content in mg/l carbonate hardness in degrees of German carbonate hardness (°dKH)

Carbonate hardness test (KH) from the very beginning in order to control assimilation of bicarbonates			
Time of installation	KH =	pH =	Date =
After 14 days	KH =	pH =	Date =
After 4 weeks	KH =	pH =	Date =
After 2 month	KH =	pH =	Date =
After 3 month	KH =	pH =	Date =
After 4 month	KH =	pH =	Date =
After 5 month	KH =	pH =	Date =
After 6 month	KH =	pH =	Date =
After 7 month	KH =	pH =	Date =
After 8 month	KH =	pH =	Date =

Bicarbonate assimilation is occurring if the KH drops and the pH is over 7.0.
More CO$_2$ helps!

6.4. Note on lighting

The lighting possibilities we enjoy in the hobby, are actually only a compromise in comparison with the light levels and colors measured in nature. The recommendations below are to be seen as guidelines concerning color temperature and strength.

The following points should be noted without fail:

1 Strength of light: 30–50 lumen per liter water (120–200 per gallon).

2 Temperature of light: mixed light, consisting of cold and warm light tubes. Recently, fluorescent lamps have been developed that have a medium kelvin temperature of 5500 and that do not need to be mixed with other lamps.

3 The recommended lighting time of 10–12 hours should not be exceeded.

4 Earlier recommendations in watt per liter have become incorrect because of the different types of lighting. »Lumen« is used to indicate the greatest light strength of all lighting methods. Only this designation is important when the lighting methods are being installed, since it shows economy and effectivity. E.g., a mercury vapor lamp has 50 lumen per watt. The metal halide lamp has 75 lumen and the Lumilux fluorescent lamp 95. If the recommendation were given in wattage, it would be X% incorrect.

5 Lumen calculation:
Previously, a Lumilux fluorescent lamp 1.5 meters long had an intake of 65 watts. Now, that figure is 58. This lamp has a light strength of 5510 lumen.

$$\frac{5510 \text{ lumen}}{58 \text{ watts}} = 95 \text{ lumen per watt}$$

6 Since the ability to penetrate the water (water column) is different for the various types of lighting, e.g. such as the mercury vapor lamp, the metal halide lamp, and the fluorescent tube, the water depth must be checked, before deciding which lamp to use. The following are in order
fluorescent tube up to 50 cm
mercury vapour lamps up to 65 cm
metal halide vapor lamps 55 to 100 cm

183

6.4. Lighting table

Aquarium size	lumen	Type of lighting/watt
70 × 45 × 35 = 110 liter	3300–5500	Mercury vapor lamps = 66–110 = 1 × 80W
		Metal halide lamp = 44–73 = none
		Fluorescent = 35–58 = 2 or 3 × 20W
100 × 50 × 40 = 200 liter	6000–10 000	Mercury vapor lamps = 120–200 = 1 × 125W or 2 × 80W
		Metal halide lamps = 80–133 = none
		Fluorescent = 63–105 = 2 × 30W or 3 x 30W
130 × 60 × 45 = 350 liter	10 530–17 550	Mercury vapor lamps = 210–351 = 3 × 80W or 2 × 125W and 1 × 80W
		Metal halide lamp = 140–234 = 1 × 150W or 2 × 150W
		Fluorescent = 110–185 = 3 × 40W or 4 × 40W
160 × 65 × 50 = 520 liter	15 600–26 000	Mercury vapor lamps = 312–520 = 4 × 80W or 3 × 125W or 4 × 125W or 3 × 125W and 1 × 80W
		Metal halide vapor lamp = 208–347 = 2 × 150W or 3 × 150W
		Fluorescent = 164–274 = 3 × 65W or 4 × 65W

6.5. Oxygen table

Oxygen saturation levels of fresh water dependent on water temperature			
Temperature in °Celsius	O_2-content per liter	Temperature in °Celsius	O_2-content per liter
5	12,4	18	9,2
6	12,1	19	9,0
7	11,8	20	8,8
8	11,5	21	8,7
9	11,2	22	8,5
10	10,9	23	8,4
11	10,7	24	8,3
12	10,4	25	8,1
13	10,2	26	8,0
14	10,0	27	7,9
15	9,8	28	7,8
16	9,6	29	7,6
17	9,4	30	7,5

6.6. Heat strength table:

Newly structured in watts by Engineer Lehmann of Darmstadt

Aquarium content in liters	Desired warmth in °Celsius above room temperature				
	2	4	6	8	10
	= necessary watt heat capacity				
20	5,5	11	16	22	27
40	8,7	17	26	35	43
60	11	23	34	45	57
80	14	27	41	55	69
100	16	32	48	64	80
120	18	36	54	72	90
140	20	40	60	80	100
160	22	44	65	87	109
180	24	47	71	94	118
200	25	51	76	101	127
220	27	54	81	108	135
240	29	57	86	114	143
260	30	60	90	121	151
280	32	63	95	127	158
300	33	66	99	133	166

The table above enables us to determine the necessary heat capacity for our aquariums. Since our aquariums generally are kept in heated rooms, with room temperatures of 18–21° C, and we usually set the aquarium temperature at 25° C, we only need 47 watts in the case of a 1 meter aquarium with 180 liter content, and a temperature difference of only 4° C between the room and the aquarium. This calculation does not take into account the necessary lighting for the tropical aquarium. If, for example, we light this aquarium with two fluorescent tubes of 30 watts each and, contrary to our recommendations (see above), the light are not ventilated and thus also warm the aquarium, an additional heat capacity of 37.5 watts results. Thus, we have a total of 84.5 watts. The aquarium is thus heated at 8° C above room temperature, or 30° C. If in addition we calculate the friction warmth of the filter hoses and the motor warmth of the pump aggregates, we see that the above still takes into account large security reserves.

An electronic thermostat takes care of the temperature regulation, e.g. Duplatherm-Digital, and keeps the water at the temperature you want it with great dependability and accuracy.

6.7. Substrate table

to facilitate the determination of filling amounts during installation

Aquarium size	Content	Layer height	Filling amount, gravel 2–3 mm Ø	Substrate additive Duplarit
70 × 45 × 35	110 liter	5 cm	15 liter	250 g
100 × 50 × 40	200 liter	7 cm	35 liter	500 g
130 × 60 × 45	350 liter	9 cm	70 liter	1000 g
160 × 65 × 50	520 liter	11 cm	115 liter	1500 g

6.8. Filter table

	Dirt capacity			Filtered out						Biological	Other
■ strong ● medium △ weak	rough	medium	fine	protein waste products	organic acids	smell	rotting and fermenting agents	coloring agents	chlor/ozone	as carrier of bacteria	duration of the filter
Dupla-High performance activated carbon	■	●	△	■	●	■	■	■	●	■	△
Filter floss	■	■	■							△	△
Trickle filter Dupla-Bioball	△	△	△	■	■	■	■			■	■

6.9. What is to be done?

Medium	Appearance	Cause	Antidote
Water in general	murky (milky)	infusoria food remains	UV lamp high performance activated carbon
	water smells	dead fish food remains	high performance activated carbon
	floating materials	general un-cleanliness	high performance activated carbon filter cotton
	water foams	too many organic substances	high performance activated carbon
	yellow water	urine products superannuated humin products	high performance activated carbon
	green, opaque, foaming water	floating algae water bloom	UV lamp
	satiny algae layer on plants, stones, slices in blue, green, reddish	smear algae redox potential too high at new installation, violet plant lamps (e.g. Grolux)	algicide algae cleanders
	brown algae layer on slices, walls, and single leaves	brown algae gravel algae (Diatoméae) too little light too much silicic acid	more light water change with plant fertilizer
	thread-like algae	too much light very good nutrient rations	algicide, less light algae clenders, molly

Medium	Appearance	Cause	Antidote
Water Chemistry	pH too high	too much aeration too little cabonic acid too light organic acids	reduce aeration CO_2 fertilization hard water soft water
	pH too low	insufficient carbonate hardness, bicarbonate assimilation acid drop	water change raise KH + GH
	carbonate hardness (KH) too low	outflow water too much aeration bicarbonate assimilation	water change with higher carbonate hardness, reduce aeration
	total hardness (GH) too low	outflow water	increase hardness with water change at higher total hardness KH + GH builders
	too little oxygen	not enough aeration, plants, light, carbon dioxide, too many fish, rotting	more light more CO_2 reduce fish, reduce food, water change, check plant fertilizer
Plants	poor growth	too little light, CO_2, nutrients, wrong substrate	more light plant fertilizer, strengthen CO_2 substrate additive »Duplarit K« heat substrate
	legthwise growth	too much red light too little light	use daylight tube (blue)
	stunted growth	too much blue too little carbon dioxide	use red light (warm tone tube) CO_2 fertilization daily fertilizer heat substrate
	yellowing of leaves	lack of iron difficulty in providing nutrients	plant fertilizer daily fertilizer more light, Fe test
	brown spots on leaves	incorrect provision of nutrients	water change, then plant fertilizer
	jagged holes on leaves	»Spitzhorn« snails	remove snails or add Puffers (snail eaters)
	Cryptocorynen rot	NO_3 too high	test water provide continuity

Medium	Appearance	Cause	Antidote
Fish	shortness of breath staying close to surface	1) lack of oxygen 2) nitrite poisoning ammonia poisoning 3) gill worms	1) measure O_2 water change and vaccination with old water NO_2^- + pH test
	mould cottonball-like covering on fins and skin	mould, bacteria	disease prevention products improve living conditions
	fringed fins red skin	bacteria	disease prevention products
	small white dots on skin and fins	ichthyophthirius	disease prevention products
	red skin small white spots like paving stones	chilodonella	disease prevention products
	covering on skin red skin partial fringing of fins	trichodina	disease prevention products
	bruised places on fins blue-yellow skin covering noticeable under diagonal light	costia	disease prevention products
	malaise timid, lack of appetite danger of infection	change in water fresh water	disease prevention products Duplagan

6.10. Glossary

acceptance	willingness to accept
acid binding capacity	to determine the alkalinity of water, equals the amount of ccm in 10 HCI, required by 100 ccm water
acid fall	rapid decrease of the pH. Occurs when water is no longer buffered. E.g. by the addition of carbonic acid or other acids. Acid binding capacity = zero
adhesion	molecular attraction exerted between the surfaces of bodies in contact
aged water	water that was highly desirable in aquariums of yesteryear, frequently yellow/ brownish. In modern aquaristics it is no longer desired.
aggressive water	contains more CO_2 than is required for the carbon dioxyde-carbonate content equilibrium. As a result the water becomes lime aggressive even attacks metal pipes.
amalgam	mercury compond
ammonia	nitrogen compond. Chemical formula NH_4, strong smelling gas consisting of nitrogen and hydrogen.
ammonium	the prefered form of nitrogen for the fertilization of submers plants.
anaerobic	process that takes place in the absence of oxygen.
antibiotica	substances produced by micro-organisms, which act to kill bacteria or inhibit their growth e.g. penicillin, streptomycin, sulfonamide etc.
antioxydants	preservatives
assimilation	in general, the uptake of nutrients by organisms to promote their own growth.
bacteria	very small, microscopic forms of life. Causative of disease in some cases.
bicarbonate	acid salts of carbonic acid
biogenic decalcification	photosynthetic dependent breakdown of bicarbonate in the water.
biotope	region uniform in environmental conditions and life
candella	luminous intensity to one sixtieth of the luminous intensity of one square centimeter of a blackbody surface of the solidification temperature of platinum.

carbonate hardness	acid binding capacity is better. Is calculated by multiplying the above by 2.8
carbon dioxyde	CO_2, also called carbonic acid
carbon dioxyde equilibrium	more correct: bicarbonate – CO_2 equilibrium. When water contains only as much carbonate and bicarbonate as the free CO_2 can keep in solution.
carbonic acid	H_2CO_3, CO_2 when in solution in water.
chelate	metal compound with a metal e.g. fe-EDTA
chelator	metal compound carrier with a metal, e.g. EDTA
chlorosis	iron deficiency causing yellowing of leaves or blanching.
colloid	substance in state of division preventing passage through a semipermeable membrane. Fails to settle and refracts light.

Color temperature	color of the light e.g. warm or cold light. Warm = larger red spectrum, cold = larger blue spectrum. Color is measured in degrees kelvin.
contra-flow	air or water circulation in opposite direction
corethra	white fly larvae
diagnosis	recognition and determination of a disease. Overall interpretation of all data e.g. water quality based on water analysis results.
EDTA	metal compound chelator. Is used as heavy metal carrier in fertilizer e.g. iron, manganese and others.
emers	above the water
free CO_2	gas which is in solution in water
glucose	widely in nature available sugar
heating capacity	heating strength in watt. Dependant on room temperature and the desired temperature. Normally 0.2 to 0.3 watt per liter.
hormone	a product of living cells that circulates in body fluids or sap.
humic acid	organic acid resulting from the decomposition of living matter.
ion exchanger	at level of electrolites. Common name given tu such devices.
iron chlorosis	iron deficiency in green leaf plants due to lack of iron in the fertilizer.
kelvin	unit for measurement of light spectra
laterite	red earth from the tropics with a high iron content.
liebig minimum law	formulated by the german chemist Liebig. The reaction is determined by the factor which is present in the smallest quantity, e.g. strong CO_2 addition achieves little if an iron deficiency exists at the same time.
light colors	light of all sources consists of a mixture of colors e.g. green, blue, red, yellow. Depending on respective amounts. Light is warm or cold. See color temperature.
lumen	luminous flux equal to the light emitted in a unit solid angle by a uniform light source of 1 candle intensity.

lux	unit of illumination that is equal to the direct light on a surface that is everywhere one meter from a uniform light source of 1 candella
manganese	metal, important trace element in the fertilization of plants
mercury vapor lamp	high presure vapor light which because of their special manufacturing process achieve a high degree of efficiency.
metal halide	has a better efficiency than the mercury vapor light. 75 lumen per watt also gives a much better spectrum that is very close to daylight
mineralisation	to transform with the help of bacteria into inorganic substances and minerals.
monoculture	cultivation of a single fruit or plant, to the exclusion of others.
nitrate	highest oxydation level of nitrogen.
nitrification	in the aquarium, the bacterial oxydation of nitrite (NO_2) to nitrate (NO_3)

nitrite	salt of HNO_2, intermediate oxydation level of nitrogen
nutrient carrier	metal compound carrier, e.g. EDTA
parameter	characteric content used to evaluate a particular group or element
pathogen	disease forming agent
pathologic	caused by or relating to a disease
phosphate	salt of orthophosphonic acid, formula PO_4. Important plant nutrient
photosynthesis	synthesis of chemical compounds with the help of radient energy. Formation of carbohydrates in the chlorophyll containing tissues of plants.
pH spread	pH values, which when surpassed will be detrimental. Different for every plant.
pH value	pondus hydrogenii. Hydrogen concentration. A number, which indicate the relative degree of acidity or alkalinity.
potassium	metal. Important plant nutrient.
Roßmäßler	Emil Adolf Roßmäßler, 1806–1867. Recognised as the father of our hobby because of 2 books »Der See im Glase« and »Das Süßwasser-Aquarium«
sedimentation	settling to the bottom of a liquid
silica stone or sand	compound of silica and at least one more element e.g. iron
submers	under water
sulfate	salt, chemical formula SO_4. Important plant nutrient.
toxic	poisonous
trace element	name given to a number of elements which are present only in very small quantities, but which are necessary to life.
virus	causative agents of infectious deseases which can multiply in living tissue very rapidly. Subcellular.

6.11. Recommended specialist literature for intensive aquaristical studies

General literature

Hans Frey	Das Aquarium von A–Z Neumann Verlag, Radebeul 1957
Hans Frey	Das Süßwasser-Aquarium Neumann Verlag, Radebeul 1972
Kosmos	Handbuch der Aquarienkunde Das Süßwasser-Aquarium Kosmos/Franckh, 1978
Werner Ladiges	Der Fisch in der Landschaft Gustav Wenzel Verlag, Braunschweig 1951
Hans J. Mayland	Große Aquarienpraxis Aquarium – Pflanzen – Fische Landbuch Verlag, Hannover 1985
Dr. Rüdiger Rühl/Hans A. Baensch	Aquarienatlas Mergus Verlag, 1985
Erich Schaller	Boshafte Aquarienkunde Kernen Verlag, Stuttgart 1970
Heinz Schöpfel	Schöne Aquarien – aber wie? Urania Verlag, Leipzig 1984
Lothar Seegers	Das Aquarium Ulmer Verlag, Stuttgart 1985
Dr. G. Sterba	Aquarienkunde I + II Verlag Zimmer & Herzog, Berchtesgaden
Hellmuth Wachtel	Aquarienhygiene Kosmos/Franckh, Stuttgart 1975

Aquarium fish

Dr. Ulrich Baensch	Kleine Zierfischkunde Tetra Verlag, Melle 1976
Burghard Kahl	Salmler im Aquarium Kosmos/Franckh, Stuttgart 1970
Horst Linke	Farbe im Aquarium: Labyrinthfische Tetra Verlag, Melle 1980
Horst Linke/Wolfgang Staeck	Amerikanische Cichliden I. Kleine Buntbarsche II. Große Buntbarsche Tetra Verlag, Melle 1984/85
Søren Neergaard	Tanganjika-Cichliden Kernen Verlag, Stuttgart 1982

Søren Neergaard	Mbuna-Cichliden Kernen Verlag, Stuttgart 1981
A. van den Nieuwenhuizen	Exoten im Aquarium Landbuch Verlag, Hannover
Werner Schmettkamp	Die Namen unserer Aquarienfische Landbuch Verlag, Hannover 1985
Lothar Seegers	Killifische – Eierlegende Zahnkarpfen im Aquarium Ulmer Verlag, Stuttgart 1980
Wolfgang Staeck/Horst Linke	Afrikanische Cichliden I. + II. Buntbarsche in West- und Ostafrika Tetra Verlag, Melle
Dr. Günther Sterba	Süßwasserfische aus aller Welt Urania Verlag, Leipzig/Jena
Günther K. H. Zupanc	Fische und ihr Verhalten Tetra Verlag, Melle 1983
A. Wheeler	Das große Buch der Fische Ulmer Verlag, Stuttgart 1977

Aquarium plants

Gerhard Brünner/Peter Beck	Neue Wasserpflanzen-Praxis Tetra Verlag, Melle 1980
C. D. K. Cook	Waterplants of the World Dr. W. Junk, The Hague, 1974
Dr. G. Friesen	Botanik für Aquarianer Kernen Verlag, Stuttgart 1953
Kaspar Horst	Pflanzen im Aquarium Ulmer Verlag, Stuttgart 1986
Helmut Mühlberg	Das große Buch der Wasserpflanzen Edition Leipzig, 1980
Niels Jacobsen	Cryptocorynen Kernen Verlag, Stuttgart 1982
N. Jacobsen/V. Hancke	Aquarienpflanzen BLV, München 1976
Kurt Paffrath	Bestimmung und Pflege von Aquarienpflanzen Landbuch Verlag, Hannover 1978
Heinz Schöpfel	Keine Probleme mit Cryptocorynen Urania Verlag, Leipzig 1975
Albert Wendt/Christel Kasselmann	Die Aquarienpflanzen in Wort und Bild, Lieferung I–XX. Kernen Verlag, Essen 1952–1985
H. C. D. de Wit	Aquariumpflanzen Ulmer Verlag, Stuttgart 1986

Water chemistry

Dr. Rolf Geisler	Wasserkunde für die aquaristische Praxis Kernen Verlag, Stuttgart 1964
Kaspar Horst/Horst Kipper	Die optimale Aquarienkontrolle aquadocumenta Verlag, Bielefeld 2. Auflage 1986

Aquarium technique

Guido Hückstedt	Aquarientechnik Kosmos/Franckh, Stuttgart 1968
Horst Overath	Aquarientechnik für die Süßwasser- und Meeresaquaristik Lehrmeister-Bücherei Nr. 45 Philler Verlag, Minden 1983

Fish diseases

K. A. Frickhinger	Gesund wie der Fisch im Wasser? Tetra Verlag, Melle 1978
Dr. H. H. Reichenbach-Klinke	Krankheiten der Aquarienfische Kernen Verlag, Stuttgart 1968
Dr. H. H. Reichenbach-Klinke	Bestimmungsbuch zur Diagnose von Fischkrankheiten F. Fischer Verlag, Stuttgart 1965
W. Schäperclaus	Fischkrankheiten Akademie Verlag, Berlin 1954
Dr. Gottfried Schubert	Krankheiten der Fische Kosmos/Franckh Verlag, Stuttgart 1964

German periodicals for fish keeping

AQUARIUM HEUTE	Das internationale Magazin für eine optimale Aquarienhaltung aquadocumenta Verlag, Bielefeld quarterly
TODAY'S AQUARIUM	The English edition of AQUARIUM HEUTE aquadocumenta Verlag, Bielefeld quaterly
TI	Aquaristik in Wort und Bild Tetra Verlag, Melle all 2 month
DATZ	Die Aquarien- und Terrarien-Zeitschrift Alfred Kernen Verlag, Essen monthly
aquarien magazin	Kosmos Verlag, Stuttgart monthly
Das Aquarium	Zeitschrift für Aquarien- und Terrarienfreunde Albrecht Philler Verlag, Minden monthly
Aquarien Terrarien	Monatsschrift für Vivarienkunde und Zierfischzucht Urania Verlag, Berlin (DDR) monthly
AquaPlanta	Informationsschrift des Arbeitskreises Wasserpflanzen im VDA quarterly
DKG-Journal	Informationsschrift der Deutschen Killifisch-Gemeinschaft all 2 month
DCG-Informationen	Informationen der Deutschen Cichliden-Gesellschaft e. V.

6.12. Subject Index

198

7. REFERENCES

7.1. Literature

Dr. Jürgen Clasen; Grundlegende Information über Algen im Süßwasseraquarium, AquaPlanta I/76.

Prof. Dr. Rolf Geisler, Futter für die Fische. I. Was fressen die Fische in der Natur? AQUARIUM HEUTE 4/84

Prof. Dr. Rolf Geisler, Futter für die Fische. II. Richtig füttern – aber wie? AQUARIUM HEUTE 2/85.

Kaspar Horst: Kohlenstoff, der wichtigste Pflanzennährstoff im Aquarium. DATZ 1976, 345, 372.

Kaspar Horst: Die Ernährung der Aquarienpflanzen. DATZ 1968, 342, 373; 1969, 22, 55.

Kaspar Horst/Horst Kipper: Die optimale Aquarienkontrolle, aquadocumenta-Verlag.

Kaspar Horst: Besserer Pflanzenwuchs durch Eisendüngung. DATZ 1965, 248.

Reinhold Kickuth: Ökonomische Leistungen höherer Pflanzen. Die Naturwissenschaften 57, 1970.

Käthe Seidel: Abbau von Bacterium coli durch höhere Wasserpflanzen. Die Naturwissenschaften 51/1964.

Käthe Seidel: Bericht an das Bundesministerium für Gesundheitswesen, 1967.

Dr. Eberhard Stengel, Algen! Die Plage der Aquarianer. AQUARIUM HEUTE Ausgabe 2/83.

Dr. Eberhard Stengel, Das Algen-Portrait. Tropische Rotalgen eine Pest?, AQUARIUM HEUTE 1/84.

Dr. Eberhard Stengel, Das Algen-Portrait. Die Grünalge Cladophora, AQUARIUM HEUTE 3/84.

Hellmuth Wachtel, Aquarium Hygiene, Kosmos-Verlag, 1963.

7. 2. Photo list

Titel and endpaper, in front and at the back:
Kaspar Horst, 2
Horst E. Kipper
Horst Linke
Gerd Siepmann

In the book:
Peter Bartmann:
169/1

Erich Dörr:
146/1

Arie de Graaf:
114/1

Dr. Hugo Herkner:
160/1, 160/2

Kaspar Horst:
21/1, 33/1, 40–41/1, 45/1, 52/1, 53/1, 53/2, 54/1, 54/2, 58/1, 59/1, 59/2, 60/1, 60/2, 61/1, 63/1, 64/2, 65/1, 67/1, 67/2, 72/1, 72/2, 72/3, 72/4, 75/1, 76/1, 78/1, 107/1, 107/2, 107/3, 109/2, 113/1, 117/2, 117/4, 117/5, 117/6, 118/1, 118/2, 118/3, 118/4, 118/5, 118/6, 119/1, 119/2, 120/1, 128/2, 147/1, 149/1, 149/2, 153/1, 166/1, 177/1

Burghart Kahl:
125/1, 125/2, 125/3, 127/1, 128/3, 131/1, 131/2

Horst E. Kipper:
14/2, 31/1, 31/2, 32/1, 32/2, 47/1, 63/1, 64/1, 69/1, 86/1, 103/1, 105/3, 105/4, 105/5, 108/1, 108/3, 125/4, 126/1, 129/3, 130/2, 132/1, 132/2, 134/1, 139/1, 142/1, 142/2, 142/3, 142/4, 143/1, 148/1, 153/3, 154/1, 154/2, 154/3, 160/1, 164/1, 171/1, 173/1, 173/2, 177/2, 177/3

Horst Linke:
128/1, 129/1, 129/2, 140/1, 163/1, 163/2, 163/3

Friedrich Möhlmann:
104/2, 108/2, 109/1, 157/1, 159/2, 165/1

Arend van den Nieuwenhuizen:
130/1, 132/3, 133/4

Kurt Paffrath:
87/1, 101/1, 102/1, 109/3, 110/1, 112–113/2, 117/1, 117/3, 121/1, 157/2, 159/1, 165/2

Michael Prasuhn:
18/1, 47/1, 49/1, 49/2, 49/3, 55/1, 55/2, 56/1, 56/2, 56/3, 57/3, 75/2, 80/1, 80/2, 81/1, 82/2, 83/1, 83/2, 85/1, 91/1, 92/1, 92/2, 93/1, 94/1, 97/1, 100/1, 100/2, 145/1, 147/2, 151/1, 151/2, 152/1, 152/2, 174/1, 174/2, 175/1, 175/2, 175/3, 178/1, 178/2

Gerd Siepmann:
82/1

Dr. Eberhard Stengel:
35/1, 36/1, 36/2, 123/2, 124/1

Tetra-Archiv:
5/1, 37/1, 121/1, 133/2, 156–157/3

W. A. Tomey:
102/2, 111/1, 121/2, 123/1

Klaus Ullrich:
114/2

Uwe Werner:
137/1, 141/1

Explantation:
The number before the oblique is the page number, the number behind is the number of the photo.

Notes

Notes

Notes